Delhi's Last Mushaira in 1845

Advance praise for the book

'Every generation needs its version of a meaningful text. When I say "text", it includes a new interpretation, a new translation, and even a new "dictionary" in tune with the changed times. Lucky are those who have more than one translator, and those who got more than one translation in a 5–10 year span are more popular than their contemporaries. Subsequent translations pose a more significant challenge even if the previous translation(s) are not up to the mark. I marvel at the courage of Ms Meenakshi Jauhari to undertake the second translation of *Dehli ki Aakhri Shama*, a historic book with an excellent translation, but we certainly need a contemporary translation. I hope that Ms Jauhari's translation surpasses the previous one, a herculean task indeed. My best wishes for her academic endeavour.'

—Dr Ather Farouqui
General Secretary, Anjuman Taraqqi Urdu (Hind)

'We live in a world of identities. Language as an arm of identity enslaves us in our cultural cocoons. Beautiful languages like Urdu enslave us more. Translation is the contraption which sets language free from within the walls of culture. If language is a caged bird, then translation is the means to break that cage. Meenakshi Jauhari's brilliant translation of *Delhi's Last Mushaira in 1845* is a sincere attempt at setting the book free for a wider audience. This wonderful translation is textual, contextual as well as intertextual. It retains Mirza Farhatullah Baig Dehlvi's cultural, linguistic, literary and historical prowess to the last full stop. Translations like this one become the embracing arms of languages.'

—Dr Shah Alam Khan
Professor, Department of Orthopaedics,
All India Institute of Medical Sciences

'A lamp glows the brightest before it dies out: *Delhi's Last Mushaira in 1845* is a window into the Mughal Empire when it was illuminated by that last burst before it was snuffed out.'

—Rana Safvi
author and historian

Delhi's Last Mushaira in 1845

A translation of

Dehli ki aakhri shama: 1261 AH mein Dehli ka ek mushaira

By Mirza Farhatullah Baig Dehlvi

Translated by Meenakshi Jauhari

AMARYLLIS

AMARYLLIS

An imprint of Manjul Publishing House Pvt. Ltd.
• C-16, Sector 3, Noida, Uttar Pradesh 201301, India
Website: www.manjulindia.com

Registered Office:
• 2nd Floor, Usha Preet Complex, 42 Malviya Nagar, Bhopal 462 003 – India

Distribution Centres
Ahmedabad, Bengaluru, Chennai, Hyderabad,
Kochi, Kolkata, Mumbai, Noida, Pune

Delhi's Last Mushaira in 1845: A translation of Dehli ki aakhri shama: 1261 AH mein Dehli ka ek mushaira by Meenakshi Jauhari

First published in paperback in India in 2025

ISBN 978-93-5543-893-5

Cover Illustration and Design: Trinankur Banerjee

Printed and bound in India by Nutech Print Services – India

Contents

Foreword

It is a privilege to write the foreword to this translation of *1261 AH mein Dehli ka ek mushaira* (or *Dehli ki aakhri shama*), the most famous mushaira in books, even though it never happened. A book which has earlier been translated requires courage in a middle-class mentality-dominated society sans literature, where nobody offends others. Only literature tells us that the vital energy of life lies in offending others and questioning them individually or their collective actions in society. Urdu litterateurs, especially Urdu poets, have done this 'crime' breathlessly. Consequently, irrespective of the merits of any predecessor translation, the new translation captures the transformation of language, a vital organ of life. As the trendsetter Urdu poet Akhtar ul-Iman said: '*Mein jab aaoonga taaza lughat humrah laaonga* (I shall bring a new dictionary)'—here, 'dictionary' certainly signifies more than a collection of words, it transcends to employ new idioms for the word, signifying life.

This translation of *Dehli ki aakhri shama* is the first complete translation of the Urdu critical edition published by Anjuman Taraqqi Urdu (Hind). It will take you through the streets of nineteenth-century Delhi and acquaint you with the greatest classical Urdu poets as they might have been in the prime of their lives.

Baig's portrait of Delhi (in the guise of a royal mushaira) was first published as an essay in 1927 in the quarterly *Urdu*, the predecessor *Urdu Adab*, published by the Anjuman and now in its 103rd year of publication. This essay took many forms and was widely read and enjoyed. It was even staged as a play, and finally, in 1991, Rasheed Hasan Khan put together an authoritative version collated from the numerous versions in circulation then. The critical edition of *Dehli ki aakhri shama* put the journey of Baig's singular work in perspective, and gave an insight into his creative process, what seeded the thought in his mind, and more.

Delhi is a rich canvas of people and their stories—it is Mir's Delhi and Ghalib's Delhi. It is also Farhatullah Baig's Delhi that he could never forsake, even though he lived almost all his adult life in Hyderabad in the Deccan. His connection with Delhi was evocatively expressed in his numerous works, and is best seen in this vivid novella set during the reign of the last Mughal Emperor.

It is also a story of Urdu, an Indian language that refuses to fade away or die under the pressure of single-minded nationalism. Translations like this reinvigorate Urdu and make its literary treasures accessible to non-Urdu readers.

—Ather Farouqui
New Delhi, August 2024

Transliteration scheme for Urdu ghazals

The ghazals here are meant to be recited aloud to relish their fullness and have a truly immersive experience of the mushaira. Consequently, I have elected to include the English transliteration of the Urdu ghazals for which I am using the following transliteration scheme which maps the Urdu and Hindi to the English.[1]

<table>
<tr><th>Urdu</th><th>Hindi</th><th>English</th></tr>
<tr><td>ا (alif)</td><td rowspan="2">अ</td><td>a / u
E.g. dam (breath), hum (we)</td></tr>
<tr><td>ع (‘ain)</td><td>’
E.g. she’r (hereon written as sher for simplicity. See note below).</td></tr>
<tr><td>آ (alif-mad)</td><td>आ</td><td>a / aa</td></tr>
<tr><td>چ (chay)</td><td>च</td><td>cha</td></tr>
<tr><td>چھ (chha)</td><td>छ</td><td>chha</td></tr>
<tr><td>د (da)</td><td>द</td><td>da</td></tr>
</table>

[1]This scheme, as an aid to pronunciation of Urdu words, is based largely on the transliteration key on the popular website *rekhta*.org, *https://www.rekhta.org/CMS/TransliterationKey*. While the transliteration key on Rekhta gives examples of English words, I have used familiar Urdu and Hindi words from the text as examples.

ڈ, ڑ (Da)	ड़, ड	Da E.g. ghaDi (moment), Dar (fear)
دھ (dha)	ध	dha
ڈھ (Dha)	ढ	Dha E.g. Dhaal (shield)
ڑھ (DHa)	ढ़	DHa E.g. baDH (increase)
گھ (gh)	घ	gha
غ (ghain)	ग़	G E.g. saaGar (wine-cup); charaaG (lamp)
ح (hay), ہ (hay-gol), ھ (hay-do chashmi)	ह	ha
خ (Khay)	ख़	KHa E.g. dozaKH (hell)
ک (kaaf)	क	ka
کھ (kh)	ख	kha
ق (qaaf)	क़	qa E.g. qariine (method)
ث (say), س (seen), ص (suad)	स	sa
ت (tay), ط (tuay)	त	ta
تھ (tha)	थ	tha
ٹ (Ta)	ट	Ta E.g. TuuTaa (break)

ٹھ (THa)	ठ	THa E.g. THokar (stumble)
ب (bay)	ब	ba
بھ (bh)	भ	bha E.g. bharye (pour)
ی (chhoti-ye), ء (hamza), zer	इ	yi / i
bari-ye ے	ए / ऐ	ye / e / ai / ei / ay E.g. maiN (me), meiN (in), paraye (strangers), dil-jale (luckless)
ج (jiim)	ज	ja
جھ (jh)	झ	jha
ذ (zaal), ز (zay), ض (zuaad), ظ (zuay)	ज़	za
ن (noon)	न	na
ں (noon-ghunna)	ँ	N E.g. insaaN (man), aaNsu (tear)
zabar	अ	a
bari-ye ے	ई	ii
pesh	उ	u
و (vao)	ओ, ऊ, औ, व	o / uu / au / v / w E.g. voh (she / he / they), maGruur (arrogant), auroN (others)

Some popular nouns such as Gaalib, sheiKH and DaaG are commonly spelt as 'Ghalib', 'sheikh' and 'Daagh' respectively. In order to minimise confusion, I have chosen—in these select cases—to deviate from the aforementioned transliteration scheme and spell the words in the way we are used to seeing them.

Other such words where I have prioritised readability over chaste representation include: 'miyaan' (in place of miyaN), 'khayaal' (in place of KHayaal), 'sukhan' (for suKHan), 'saans' (instead of saaNs), and 'Khuda' (for KHuda).

Finally, throughout the book, the commonly recognised spellings of 'ghazal' (in place of Gazal), 'rekhta' (instead of reKHta) and 'sher' (instead of she'r) have been retained.

Translator's introduction

Mirza Farhatullah Baig Dehlvi's immortal classic, *Delhi's Last Mushaira in 1845* (henceforth referred to as *Last Mushaira*) is the portrait of a historical-fictional mushaira in the Mughal city of Delhi in the mid-nineteenth century, an inflection point in the history of the city.

The mid-nineteenth century was a time when the Mughal Badshah Bahadur Shah Zafar was left with no real powers and no real empire to rule over. Already in his mid-sixties when he came to the throne in 1837, Zafar was a badshah in name only. The British had gradually usurped more and more of his powers, removing his name from coins, ending the long-standing tradition of giving the Emperor the ceremonial gift or nazr,[1] and finally, even taking control of Delhi. Zafar's real authority lay only within the walls of the Lal Qila (Red Fort) and that too was in some ways pinched. Not only was he at the mercy of the British for a paltry stipend that fell despairingly short of the royal expenses, but the British Resident also kept a close eye on the Badshah's actions and decisions.[2] What rankled most was

[1]Nazr was customarily presented to the Emperor as an acknowledgement of his divine authority. With the steep erosion of Mughal power in the first quarter of the nineteenth century, many things changed, and in September 1837, when Bahadur Shah ascended the throne, nazr was presented to the Emperor by the East India Company (EIC) for the very last time.

[2]The British Resident initially acted as the Governor General's ambassador to the Mughal court, but as British power grew, he assumed the role of the Governor of Delhi and its surroundings. The Emperor could not give gifts or robes of honour

that Zafar did not even have the authority to appoint his own successor. Still, no power on earth could change the fact that he was still the Mughal Badshah who had the moral authority and charisma, and whom the inhabitants of Delhi looked up to, especially when faced with difficulties.[3] And so, despite all the humiliations, Zafar remained a much-loved guardian on one level and a cultural icon on another.

As a person, Bahadur Shah Zafar was singularly talented with high literary and aesthetic tastes. An accomplished poet, the ghazals he composed in Urdu and Persian are sung to this day; he also wrote in Arabic, Braj Bhasha and Punjabi, producing a volume of poetry in each of the four languages, barring Arabic. He was known to be a skilled calligrapher and a patron of miniature painters and creators of gardens. As a reputed Sufi scholar and teacher, he took on murids (students). Alongside all his intellectual attainments, Zafar was also acknowledged as an excellent rider, archer and swordsman, and despite his advanced years, remained a crack shot with the rifle. Above all, Bahadur Shah was a great patron of literature and the arts. His patronage and catalysing influence contributed to making this epoch historic—it would

---

to noblemen outside the territory of Delhi without the British Resident's nod. He had to make an application to British courts to get rent from his own lands. The Badshah was also obstructed from presenting jewels from the crown jewels to his family members without first informing the Resident, and occasionally, even made to ask for 'unauthorised' gifts to be returned if the Resident got to know of it. William Dalrymple, *The Last Mughal: The Fall of a Dynasty*, Delhi, 1857, pp. 37–38.

[3]There were instances when Bahadur Shah interceded with the British Resident on behalf of the people—for instance, when washermen were prohibited from using a section of the Yamuna bank that they had been customarily using for the washing and drying of clothes, or when a kebab-seller near Hauz Qazi was told to remove his stall from where he had been selling his kebabs for years. One time, a visitor from America who had been robbed, approached the Emperor for help, and the latter gave him a horse and ten rupees for his expenses. Amar Farooqui, *Zafar and the Raj:Anglo-Mughal Delhi c. 1800–1850*, pp. 108–09.

later come to be known as the Delhi Renaissance—with an exceptional and unmatched flourishing of Urdu poetry.

Bahadur Shah's court was the nucleus for cultural and literary luminaries of the period. Among its brightest stars were the celebrated poets Mirza Ghalib and his equally famous adversary Sheikh Ibrahim Zauq, Poet Laureate of Delhi and the Badshah's teacher.[4] Also decorating the Lal Qila were several other notable intellectuals—Maulvi Imam Bakhsh Sehbai, Maulana Mamluk Ali and Mufti Sadruddin Aazurda, Sadr Amin (chief judge) of Delhi.[5]

It was truly an era of all-round blossoming: we see, for instance, the rise of Shah Waliullah, acclaimed Islamic scholar who translated the Quran into Persian, and his distinguished son Shah Abdul Aziz Dehlvi, widely renowned for his knowledge of the hadith, fiqh (Islamic jurisprudence), history, mathematics and logic, along with poetry and literature.[6] The Delhi College was a hub for cultural activities and scholarly pursuits, and boasted of teachers like Dr Chaman Lal, one of Zafar's personal physicians, and Master Ramchandra, a talented mathematics professor. The patronage of the court also enlivened the Delhi school of

---

[4]Please see *Appendix B* for brief biographies of these master poets.

[5]Indeed, the Lal Qila or Qila, as it was popularly called, was the soul of the city and exerted great influence on the life of ordinary citizens, whether in matters of culture and fashion trends, or for the latest gossip, or even a popular poet's newly-minted ghazal. Everyone was connected to the Qila in one way or another. According to Mirza Ghalib, the social and cultural life of Delhi centred around five things: the Red Fort, Chandni Chowk, Jama Masjid, Yamuna and the famous festival known as 'Phoolwalon ki sair'. K.A. Nizami (trans.), Ather Farouqui, *Delhi in Historical Perspectives*, pp. 87–88.

[6]Shah Abdul Aziz Dehlvi was a widely respected teacher and had pupils across the country. Profoundly wise, he saw no difference in referring to God as 'Allah' or 'Parmeshwar'. He favoured learning English and welcomed the Western advances in science; at the same time, he exhorted people against foreign domination. Ibid, p.72.

painting with gifted painters like Raja Jivan Ram, Husain Nazir and Mazhar Ali Khan, one of Zafar's favourites. This Delhi was not only home to the great educationist and reformer Sir Syed Ahmad Khan, it was also an irresistible magnet for someone like the young student Karimuddin Magfoor, who came from Panipat to be able to study in Delhi College, and whom we shall meet further on. New developments in Western science were being translated into Persian and Arabic for the first time, and there was an air of open-mindedness and intellectual stimulation all around.[7] What is outstandingly magnified, however, was the great flowering in Urdu poetry, an unforgettable coming of age that especially illuminates this patch of Delhi's history.

The great Uprising of 1857—which would have British guns lay waste to the city in order to crush the rebelling Indian troops, and in the process, forever change its civilisational fabric—was still twelve years away in the future, and the decade was pregnant with all kinds of possibilities for a Delhi suffused with the excitement of achieving ever greater heights.

When in the 1920s, Farhatullah Baig crafts a historic-fictional mushaira, this is the era of fullness he is harking back to; a time when poetry was in the very air one breathed, and was everyone's province, regardless of class, caste, occupation and education. It was a time when reciting ghazals of a living poet was the greatest tribute, and when dead poets mingled freely with the living, in a manner of speaking, through the medium of their poetry.

---

[7]In the early 1850s, Delhi, at the height of intellectual and cultural vibrancy, boasted of six famous madrasas and at least four smaller ones, nine newspapers in Urdu and Persian, five intellectual journals published from the Delhi College and several printing presses and publishers. William Dalrymple, *The Last Mughal: The Fall of a Dynasty*, Delhi, 1857, p.95.

Baig's writing draws from a profound sense of nostalgia and a desire to return to the 'old' Delhi of the mid-nineteenth century. By the 1920s, British influence has irrevocably altered the city, and Baig no longer knows the Delhi that meets his eye. This transformation of Delhi was not merely a physical alteration or a skin-deep modernisation; rather, it was a transmutation of an altogether different nature.[8] It was an intricate and deeply intertwined political and cultural juggernaut that had begun rolling in 1857, and whose momentum was still continuing, unstopped, unabated.

On the morning of 11 May 1857, rebelling Hindu and Muslim troops arrived in Delhi from Meerut and took control of the palace and the city's administration and defence. They held out against the British forces gathering on the city's periphery through the blazing summer that year. On 14 September 1857, however, after four months, British troops finally marched into Delhi. A week later, they managed to suppress the rebel Indian soldiers, and on 21 September, Bahadur Shah was taken prisoner. Anarchy reigned, homes and shops were wantonly destroyed, libraries were burnt down, citizens were killed and even the doyens of art and culture, teachers and poets were not spared. The beating heart of Delhi was now on life support.[9] The city's

---

[8]After the Uprising, many of the buildings in the city were either used by the British as barracks or were razed to the ground. The palace was used as a British garrison, the Diwaan-e Aam was turned into a hospital and all the exquisite buildings south of the Diwaan-e Khaas were considered suitable only for the use of British troops. Only the Diwaan-e Khaas itself was seen as worth preserving based on its architectural merit. During 1860, all buildings within a radius of 448 yards from the Red Fort walls were authorised for demolition, including the Akbarabadi Mosque. Percival Spear, *Twilight of the Mughuls: Studies in Late Mughul Delhi*, pp. 221–22.

[9]For more on the 1857 Uprising and its aftershocks, see Amar Farooqui, *Zafar and the Raj: Anglo-Mughal Delhi c. 1800–1850*, Chapters 7 and 8.

poets were forced to flee the city and rebuild their world under new skies—Mirza Ghalib, Daagh, Rasa, Taskeen, Shaghil and Haya sought employment at Rampur, either living there, or like Ghalib, travelling between Delhi and Rampur. Many others like Altaf Husain Hali, Aziz Mirza and Mehdi Ali Mohsinul Mulk, found their way to Hyderabad. And thus was stamped out the exuberant and short-lived Delhi Renaissance.[10] Among the thousands that escaped the ravaged city was one of Baig's heroes, Muhammad Husain Azad, whose presence we feel on every page of *Last Mushaira.* Summarily evicted from his home on bayonet point, Azad fled with his family to Lahore.

In the decades that followed, the political masters stepped up the cultural wing of their colonising project as they sought to subjugate not just the body, but also the soul of a vibrant civilisation. A key dimension of this remodelling was the discrediting of Urdu and Persian poetry, and the push for its reform in the image of literary naturalism that was sweeping across England in the nineteenth century. These efforts were of course undergirded by the colonialist belief that Victorian aesthetics, sensibilities and morality were 'superior'. In the new order, just about everything in Urdu and Persian poetry was deemed 'wrong'—the way it was documented, its creative register and more. Criticism was especially heaped on its substance, its picturesque themes of love and separation, beloved and beauty, nightingale and garden, that stood in sharp contrast to the 'natural poetry' trend in the West.

Writing in the early twentieth century, in an essay on the changing face of Delhi entitled 'Nai Dehli,'[11] Farhatullah Baig

---

[10]C.F. Andrews writes, 'The renaissance at Delhi gave a sudden illumination to the age.... Light flickered and leapt up for a brief moment before it died away.' Andrews goes on, 'More than any other single cause, the Mutiny killed it.' Frances W. Pritchett, *Nets of Awareness: Urdu Poetry and its Critics*, p. 15.

[11]*Mazameen-e Farhatullah Baig: Intekhab https://www.rekhta.org/ebooks/mazameen-e-farhatullah-beg-intekhab-ebooks/#270*

makes a scathing observation:

> And have you heard the language spoken here? Subhanallah! What *is* it? And then, we go about proudly claiming that Urdu is our tongue! I can't say about Lucknow, but yes, Dehli's language has donned a new look. It's unbelievable, the words I get to hear. And these educated people have ruined it even more—one word of Urdu followed by two words of English. I have begun to despise this new tongue!

Farhatullah goes on:

> My life is spent, a small part is left. I wake up in the morning and after my namaaz, go up to Mehdiyan cemetery, or sometimes to the cemetery at Kallu ka Takiya. Resting there are the people who lived in the old Dehli.[12] I go there, sit by their graves, shed a tear or two in their memory and in the memory of their Dehli. My heart feels lighter. As evening falls, I go and sit on the steps of the Jama Masjid, watch the sights and ponder the tamasha of God's creation. What Dehli was, and what it has become!

Baig's mushaira is, thereby, the portrait of a city and a way of life that now solely exists in the collective memory of 'Dehli-wallahs'; indeed, the *Last Mushaira* reads as a powerful urge to record the city's older face in photographic detail, so that the images could perhaps be restored to future generations that would come farther down the river of time, in some unseen and uncertain future.

---

[12]The Mehdiyan cemetery is situated near Maulana Azad Medical College, Delhi Gate. Hakim Momin Khan, preeminent poet of Mughal Delhi who also features prominently in the mushaira, is buried here. Also interred here are Shah Waliullah, his father Shah Abdur Rahim, as well as the scholar Mamluk-ul Ali who is seen at the mushaira.

Baig and Muhammad Husain Azad

In his preface of *Last Mushaira*, Baig states, '…an idea bubbled up in my mind that, like Muhammad Husain Azad's mehfil of poets in his *Nairang-e khayaal*, I too should institute a mushaira….'

Farhatullah indeed drew his inspiration from Muhammad Husain Azad (1830–1910). A Dehli-wallah from an earlier generation, Azad was a gifted and influential scholar and writer. His father, Maulvi Muhammad Baqir, had set up the *Dehli Urdu Akhbar*, Delhi's first Urdu newspaper, in 1836-37. Azad received his education at Delhi College in the Urdu-medium Oriental section. By the 1850s, he was assisting his father in his newspaper work, which continued through the Uprising. When Delhi fell in September 1857, twenty-seven-year-old Azad was forced to flee with his wife and infant daughter. His father was executed by the British on suspicion of helping the rebel soldiers, and his one-year-old daughter succumbed to a stray bullet during the family's flight from Delhi. After years of wandering aimlessly, heartbroken and desperate, Azad finally reached Lahore in 1861. A relative helped him get a low-level job in the postmaster general's office in the city. The founding of Lahore's Government College in 1864 with Gottlieb Wilhelm Leitner as its principal was a turning point for Azad, who was tutoring the Englishman in Urdu at that time. Leitner set up the Anjuman-e Punjab[13] soon after, and made Azad a part of it. Azad threw himself into it, working hard to

[13]The Anjuman-e Punjab had prominent British officials and Muslim, Hindu and Sikh intellectual elites of the region as its members. With its diverse membership, the Anjuman became the centre for intellectual and social reform in the region. It arranged public lectures, set up a free library and reading room, compiled educational texts and translations in Indian languages and later established Lahore's famous Oriental College. The body turned out to be a great success, and became a template for similar societies in other major cities. In 1866, Azad became a lecturer on behalf of the Anjuman; in 1867, he became its secretary. Frances W. Pritchett, *Nets of Awareness: Urdu Poetry and its Critics*, p. 32.

shore up the body's credibility with his lectures and papers. Of the 142 papers the Anjuman published in total, twenty-two were authored by Azad.

Between 1875 and 1877, Azad wrote *Nairang-e khayaal* (*The Wonder World of Thought*), which was published later in 1880. It was a set of thirteen essays, most of them by Samuel Johnson and Joseph Addison, that Azad transcreated in Urdu. These were introduced by two prefatory essays in which Azad expanded upon the basic themes of 'new poetry', as it was being introduced then in the Indian intellectual sphere.

That same year, Azad also published his acclaimed masterpiece, *Aab-e hayat* (*Water of Life*). Regarded as the first chronological history of Urdu poetry, it is perhaps the most widely read Urdu book in the past centuries. To this day, it remains an important sourcebook for historical theories of Urdu poetry, descriptions of the poets and their interactions with their peers and pupils, samples of poetic compositions, as well as anecdotes that bring to life the poet as a person.[14]

Of course, both these works by Azad exerted a profound influence on Baig when he was constructing the *Last Mushaira*.

Farhatullah Baig and Azad, literary icons of their respective eras, shared striking similarities in how their lives panned out. They lived in Delhi about half a century apart, and both left the city when they were in their twenties—Azad was rudely thrown out in the aftermath of the Uprising, while Baig left in 1907 in search of a livelihood. Both had a deep affinity for Delhi and wrote extensively about its vibrantly distinctive culture. Significantly, even while being employed with the British government and well informed of Western literary trends, these Dehli-wallahs never really gave up their own literary taste and retained their passion

[14]It is available in English, having been translated and edited by Frances W. Pritchett in association with Shamsur Rahman Faruqi; *Aab-e hayat: Shaping the Canon of Urdu Poetry*, Oxford University Press, New Delhi, 2003.

for the old Urdu poetic tradition right until the end of their lives. They nursed an unrelenting hunger to return to the city of their birth and youth; they never did. Azad died in Lahore in 1910, and Baig was interred in Hyderabad in 1947.

Azad stood at the stormiest point of the British project of cultural westernisation, canvassing for the reform of Urdu poetry, but inwardly regretful of the slow death of the old poetic tradition. Roughly half a century later, Baig found himself standing in the deepening twilight of Urdu and the final sundown of a whole way of life. And he was besieged by wistful remembrances of Mughal Delhi, braided with a sense of abiding pride in the living tradition of Urdu.[15]

Baig crafts the Last Mushaira

Baig's work was first published in July 1927 as a muraqqa' (essay) in *Urdu*, a quarterly published by Anjuman Taraqqi Urdu (Hind). In 1928, journalist and prose writer Khwaja Hasan Nizami published it in book form with the title *Dehli ki aakhri shama.* Over time, it was included in many courses of study, and for more than fifty years, it was part of various curricula. It was also included in the first volume of *Mazameen-e-Farhat* (first edition, Hyderabad), in which Baig made some revisions and gave it the title, *1261 AH mein Dehli ka ek mushaira.*[16]

The story begins with Karimuddin Magfoor, a young maulvi from Panipat, just graduated from the Delhi College, setting up a printing press in Hauz Qazi. Karimuddin is a historical figure

---

[15]Farhatullah Baig had studied at the Hindu College and later graduated from St Stephen's College. He had received a Western education, but was also well-versed in Arabic and Urdu, and had a keen appreciation for literature and culture. See also, Rasheed Hasan Khan's preface in *Appendix A*.

[16]1261 AH (Anno Hegirae) or Hijri calendar, corresponding to the year 1845 in the Gregorian calendar.

who wrote many books and made Delhi his home. To invigorate his fledgling business, Karimuddin wishes to publish a tazkirah,[17] for which he believes a mushaira would be a good idea. It would give him access to the city's poets and their kalaam. And indeed, in that era, the mushaira was a forum for the presentation of new poets and new work. It was how poets and their creations caught the popular imagination.

The creative license that Baig takes is in the number of poets included in the mushaira. Whereas Karimuddin's mushaira had been limited to a few select poets, Baig brings in almost all the prominent poets of the time. He adds another level of authentic detail by talking to people who had known the earlier Delhi. He constructs faces and describes people based on these actual conversations, while also corroborating other pieces of information he gets from his interactions.

On the flip side, historians sound a cautionary note against some of the literary liberties Baig has taken. For instance, the Emperor's ghazal would not be recited at Karimuddin's mushaira as it was against royal protocol for the Badshah's ghazal to be recited anywhere else but at a royal mushaira.[18] Ultimately, for a truly rewarding read, the reader's lens should neither be a chaste historical lens nor for that matter, a purely fictional one. The *Last Mushaira* is not a critical essay or a scholarly treatise, and it is also not a tale of fantasy spun out of thin air. The book should be seen as an attempt to breathe life into a slice of nineteenth-

---

[17]The tazkirah is a traditional genre of literary anthology in Persian and Urdu. It contains brief selections from the works of various poets, with some introductory comments about each poet; it targets an audience of insiders. In essence, a tazkirah is a textual extension of a mushaira.

[18]Indeed, regular mushairas were held in the Diwaan-e Aam at the Emperor's bidding on the fifteenth and twenty-ninth of every month. These were later discontinued. Ali Khan Mahmudabad, *Poetry of Belonging: Muslim Imaginings of India 1850–1950*, p. 49.

century Delhi with its singular ambience, through the medium of a royal mushaira boasting of poets in stylish attires. On display are their mannerisms, their interactions with one another and the cultural nuances of the time.

In the voice of Karimuddin, Farhatullah relates the events as they unfold—the planning and invitations, the preparations and then the mushaira itself. Especially fascinating is the account of Karimuddin's audience with the Mughal Badshah. Here, Baig could have given the reader a peek into the grand formality of Bahadur Shah Zafar's durbar, even if that were tawdry when compared with his Mughal ancestors' magnificent courts. But rather, Baig chooses to draw back the curtain on the Badshah in a personal, even intimate setting—a more insightful portrayal by all counts. It's a picture of dimmed lights and lost glories as Zafar's old age and vulnerability are evident even though not explicitly highlighted. For us in the present, it is tempting to believe that Farhatullah makes his creative choice with the benefit of hindsight, from across a gap of about eighty years, and from a point where he acknowledges that Zafar fostered a remarkable renaissance in Urdu poetry. At the same time, Baig cannot help but subtly suggest that ultimately Zafar proved incapable of safeguarding his throne—with disastrous results for the Mughal dynasty, and indeed, all of Hindustan.

After getting the Badshah's blessings, as was the customary practice, Karimuddin goes to the homes of the key poets to invite them to the mushaira: Ustad Zauq, Mirza Ghalib, Hakim Momin Khan, Nawab Mustafa Khan Shefta and Sadruddin Aazurda. The venue for the mushaira is carefully chosen and given a thorough makeover in view of the fact that the Heir Apparent Mirza Fakhru and other princes from the Qila will be in attendance. The reader sees garlands of flowers, lights of all kinds and a profusion of fragrances—a veritable sensory feast.

When the mushaira is in progress, Karimuddin is the proverbial fly on the wall: a talking fly with an opinion and a keen eye, one that addresses the reader directly. He gives bemused accounts of a father complaining about his rather 'forward' son for following the Lucknow style of language (and dress), a minor princeling and his whimsies, and more. Every poet's face that the ceremonial lamp illuminates, is put in the spotlight by Karimuddin's lively narration.

Baig also adds a visual to show the seating arrangement at the mushaira: a large rectangle, not unlike a grand dining table, with poets seated all around. At the head is the royal seat of the Heir Apparent and Mir-e-mushaira,[19] Mirza Fakhru.

It is noteworthy that Baig's historical-fictional mushaira brings together a large number of poets from across the spectrum of society. The Qila princes rub shoulders with humble working-class poets; ustads of rekhta are seated alongside a bright-eyed college student; Ghalib's French student recites his ghazal, as does an octogenarian poet; and somewhat unexpectedly, there's a soldier too, proudly attired in his military uniform. The poets are not all from Delhi. There is a poet from Secunderabad in the Deccan, one from faraway Madras and yet another one from Rampur. And so, we see poets of all hues, classes, ages and from various regions seated together in the glorious democracy of a nineteenth-century poetry symposium. One of the stars of the evening is the seventeen-year-old Nawab Mirza Khan Daagh Dehlvi, accompanying the Heir Apparent, Mirza Fakhru. Daagh Dehlvi would go on to be celebrated as one of the brightest pearls in the ocean of Urdu poetry and one of the last great poets of the old Delhi school. Sadly, it is entirely a man's world and there is no woman poet present in the mushaira; at this time, women would not be present at any mushaira held anywhere.[20]

---

[19]Mir-e-mushaira refers to the person who acts as the presider of the symposium.

[20]It wasn't like women did not compose any poetry at all; in the Deccan, we know

Baig takes yet another poetic liberty, and that is, having two ceremonial lamps instead of the customary single lamp. The circulation of two lamps, in turns, is to ensure that all poets are given equal importance and no one feels disrespected.

The mushaira progresses through the night, the mood waves rising and falling and then inching up again as the ceremonial lamps circulate from one poet to the next. Each poet has a signature style of delivery that is part and parcel of the performance. Some recite their ghazals in tarannum, singing them like a song; some prefer taht ul-lafz, literally spoken or recited poetry; still others explain the couplets as if giving a lesson to their pupils. Every poet's recitation is followed by words of praise from the gathering. Notice too, the etiquette for giving praise during or after a ghazal recitation—its nuances are most telling. Newbie poets, those who are just starting out on their literary adventures, are given unstinted praise, avuncular advice even, to assure them, pat their backs and set them firmly on their road. But a mature poet whose work is drawn from a deeper deliberation and displays greater ripeness, is accorded well-considered approbation. The appreciation comes from contemporaries—they have a sound understanding of the ustad's kalaam and its deeper connections in the poetic universe. The younger poets respectfully listen to learn.[21] The expert poet does not expect effusive praise—in fact,

---

of Lutfunnissa Imtiaz and Mah Laqa Chanda Bai, who had published their poetry divans in 1796 CE and 1797 CE respectively. In Delhi, there was the refined and celebrated Wazir Khanum, also known as Chhoti Begum, mother of Nawab Mirza Khan Daagh Dehlvi, who wrote under the pen name 'Zuhra'. She is, however, not known to have published any divan. There would most certainly have been other women poets too. In about a century's time, women would become visible in mushairas held in cities like Delhi and Bombay; there would be women-only mushairas as well, and women unable to attend these gatherings would send in their entries via post to be recited by others.

[21]Mushairas were like poetry workshops for young budding poets—listening to masters of rekhta as they recited their ghazals that drew upon a rich repertoire of themes,

he might be offended if he's given undeserved applause. Expert that he is, he knows exactly which couplet merits an ecstatic wah-wah and Subhan-allah!

This translation: Fusion of horizons

When Baig wove his mushaira, he was directing it to future generations. This complete translation is a step in that direction, and enlarges the scope of the conversation Baig started about a century ago. It takes a fresh view of this timeless work, forging a unique covenant with the Delhi that was.

This translation is based on the critical edition by Anjuman Taraqqi Urdu (Hind), sixth edition, 2015, restored and edited by Rasheed Hasan Khan in 1991, on the basis of the original text published in the *Urdu* (1927) and Baig's revised version included in *Mazameen-e-Farhat*.[22]

Taking a step back to take a quick look at an earlier translation: the previous translation[23] was notable in that it brought this Urdu classic to the English-reading audience. It is, however, more than forty years old now. And there are lacunae in it that detract from the totality of the experience that Farhatullah Baig wished to give his readers. For instance, Baig brings in rekhti poets and their ghazals with their distinctive feminine voice; these are absent in the

---

noting down select couplets in their notebooks, understanding the employment of metaphors for clarifying an idea or for embellishment, and much more.

[22]Please see *Appendix* A for Rasheed Hasan Khan's deeply insightful preface to the 1991 edition. A great twentieth century scholar of Urdu, Rasheed Hasan Khan was widely respected for his unmatched contribution to Urdu orthography, research, textual analysis and editing of classical Urdu texts. See also, for life and contributions of Rasheed Hasan Khan: *https://aws-static.iicdelhi.in/s3fs-public/2022-10/IICQ_Autumn_2022_web.pdf*

[23]Akhtar Qamber (trans.), *The Last Mushai'rah of Dehli*, Orient Longman Pvt. Ltd., 1979.

earlier translation. The poet Muhammad Ali Tishna arrives naked and inebriated, and remains so until his exit from the mushaira after having recited his ghazal. His state of undress is as much a part of the mehfil as is the regal attire of Mirza Fakhru. In the previous translation, while Tishna and his ghazal are included, his unclothed state is glossed over.[24] In his original work, Baig liberally uses footnotes to sprinkle colour in the portrait he paints of Delhi. Two long and exquisitely detailed footnotes, however, are conspicuously absent in the previous translation: the first, on the sartorial styles in vogue then, and the second, an account of a full-house wrestling match in the heart of the city. Also missing is a particularly personalised footnote wherein Baig says he actually saw poet Momin Khan's house and the low parapet wall that was the cause of his untimely death. Finally, the last chapter, 'Taqdeer', that wraps up Karimuddin's story is also absent.

This translation utilises recent historical sources, enabling the reader to gain a rich perspective of the time and the place the mushaira is set in. It is in line with Baig's objective to showcase their finely textured world and way of living, complete with all its mores and manners. All of Baig's original footnotes have been included herein, and wherever Baig employs the first person in the notes, it is explicitly called out.

I would also like to point out that in the original text, the city is called 'Dehli', and I have, therefore, retained this in the translation; arising from this is the quintessential 'Dehli-wallah'. However, in the footnotes and other places, I call it 'Delhi' as we know it today.

---

[24]It was Tishna's usual style to be found in a state of inebriation and undress. Shamsur Rahman Faruqi writes of another gathering that Tishna is part of, '...there was among the audience the distinguished young poet Mir Muhammad Ali Tishna. His days of inebriety and perhaps a little madness or "absorption" were just beginning. He went about very nearly unclothed, and often came to assemblies of poets or coffee houses, but rarely took part in any discussion. His wits were entirely sharp and his brain fully active.' Shamsur Rahman Faruqi, *The Mirror of Beauty*, p. 753.

And now, for the translation itself—it was a process of weighing between tracing the Urdu text to be faithful to Baig's vision and telling, and making it compatible with contemporary readers' preferences. In the end, it was an instinctive harmonising between the two—a bringing to life, authentically. I have tried to retain the formality that characterised the spoken language of the period without overburdening the narration with unnatural frills. Also, Baig's writing has a flow, and then occasionally, he dives into the depths with a deftness that keeps the reader engrossed while ensuring they don't lose their mooring. It has been my sincere endeavour to carry over this smoothness to the narration in English. The translation of the ghazals and couplets merited a careful calibration and balancing of voice, and sometimes my literary choices changed dramatically from one day to the next. As a matter of fact, poetic motifs in Urdu poetry do not carry over to English in a seamless way. Even so, it was a fascinatingly creative act as I attempted to evoke the punch of an Urdu line or couplet, or sought to explore and expand the garland of English language metaphors to be a mirror to the original; in a sense, crossing the sensory bridge step by step across the linguistic divide, trying, all the while, to put together a garden somewhat as lovely as the magnificent bagh on the other side.

Ultimately, my aim has been to ensure that each ghazal translation speaks in its own voice and with an internal rhythm, so as to be a good fit for oral recitation. Only then can the lucky reader hope to catch a glimpse of the mushaira in progress and delight in the delicate figments of the poet's universe. Which is what Farhatullah had in mind, as he wishes aloud, '...almost as if the reader were present in their midst (in the mehfil)... delighting in the lyrical cadences, dramatic pauses, and play in their reciting voices....' In my translation of the ghazals, I have followed the first, second or third person usages as they are in the original. Quranic references have been retained, as also the presence of the lovers' comrade and confidant, the saqi. In the end, it is the reader who will decide if the ghazals sing the song of their poets, and if their lost world is animated in the process.

Along with the English translations I have also included the transliterated Urdu ghazals; please refer to the transliteration table (on page ix). Above all, the joy of a ghazal is in reciting it aloud!

Appendix A of the book contains the translation of Rasheed Hasan Khan's deeply insightful preface that situates this work in the appropriate historical and literary context, while also tracing its life-journey through various stages and forms of publication. *Appendix B* contains sketches of the master poets of Delhi in that era: Sheikh Mohammad Ibrahim Zauq, Mirza Asadullah Khan Ghalib and Hakim Momin Khan Momin. These are for the benefit of the reader who may not be familiar with these stalwarts.

End of an era

In the times that followed, in their individual lives, the poets featured in this historic-fictional mushaira went back to working the mill of life, each after his own fashion. Uprooted from their beloved Delhi in the aftershock of the Uprising, a few cobbled together a life in other cities, shadows of happier times, while some perished and a few were lost in the maelstrom, never to be seen again.

In the years to come, the royal mushaira with its sparkle and splendour faded, giving way to literary gatherings of other kinds. It wasn't that mushairas died out completely; instead, they became either small intimate gatherings held in towns and qasbas or at holy shrines, or large-scale political ones hosted by political parties. Their form changed, their subject matter changed, their audience changed. As printing technology became widespread, newspapers, pamphlets and other printed material gained popularity, and that in turn, ensured that poetry and poetic ideas gained readers across different regions. It also encouraged other kinds of engagement with poetry, like discussions, criticisms, reviews and debates or even rebuttals.

In the twentieth century, mushairas often became spaces to transmit social and political messages to larger, more diverse audiences. Mushairas also began to be organised in educational institutions. They were even held as part of conferences and gatherings. Other mediums of mass communication came to be employed, radio mushairas being one such popular format. In a sense, poetry walked out to be among the masses and talked to people in their everyday tongues (circling back to when poetry was the common man's daily fare). That, however, is another story.[25]

Baig's mushaira of 1845 ends with a moving nazm by the royal teacher, Sheikh Mohammad Ibrahim Zauq, just as dawn is breaking. It is the end of the last mushaira of Delhi.

But the mushaira lives on…

---

[25]For a comprehensive understanding of the mushaira, its elements, evolution and its connection with the Indian milieu, see Ali Khan Mahmudabad, *Poetry of Belonging: Muslim Imaginings of India* 1850–1950.

Delhi's Last Mushaira in 1845

Farhatullah Baig's preface (1927)

naam-e nek-e raftgaaN zaa'ye makuun
taa ba-maanad naam-e nekat barqaraar[26]

Forget not the good deeds of people of the past
So that you are remembered for your good deeds in the future.

Ghalib, the immortal poet of Dehli, has said, 'Man is a tumult of thoughts.' But for a thought to produce any consequence or result, an external catalyst is needed. Man's mind is a treasure trove of ideas, and to unlock this treasure trove, what is ultimately needed is a tangible key located in the material world. Right from my childhood, I was passionately interested in knowing about Urdu poets and their lives and times. But never was there any inducement to birth the idea to bring together the journeys of Urdu poets in one place, and then to express that idea in the form of vivid life-like word pictures.

When something is meant to be, however, compulsions and motives present themselves, on their own and quite naturally. Is it not a coincidence that I found a hand-drawn sketch of Hakim Momin Khan 'Momin' Dehlvi in an old stack of papers? And no sooner had I found this than an idea bubbled up in my

[26]These are the last two lines of a four-line verse by renowned Persian poet, Saadi Shirazi (1210–1291 CE).

mind that, like Muhammad Husain Azad's mehfil of poets in his *Nairang-e khayaal*, I too should institute a mushaira. But rather than critique or comment upon the poets' poetry, I should only faithfully mirror their walking and talking pictures.

Little by little, the idea gained ground, became solid and presented in my mind's eye a portraiture of a gathering of poets. However, I was still not sure about how to bring together the poets from different eras in one place. This problem too found a happy resolution in this sher of Amirullah Tasleem:[27]

javaani se zyaada vaqt-e piirii josh hotaa hai
bhaDaktaa hai charaaG-e sub.h jab KHaamosh hotaa hai

Old age has more passion than the years of youth bygone
The night lamp flares with brilliance in the hush of dawn.

The fortuitous remembering of this sher all at once brought to my mind a vision of the last phase of Dehli poets and poetry. I gained clarity that in place of the entire galaxy of Urdu poets, I would concentrate on the final phase of poetic efflorescence in Dehli.

It seemed befitting—a man on his deathbed often displays a renewed flicker of life before finally succumbing. In Bahadur Shah Zafar's Dehli, Urdu poetry too showed an energised flicker of revival. For Zafar was Emperor in name only. By the time he ascended the Mughal throne, the treasury was empty and the British gave him a miserly stipend that barely covered the expenses of the Qila. In striking contrast, kingdoms in the Deccan and Awadh were awash with rivers of wealth. Regardless, the glitter

[27]Munshi Amirullah Tasleem was born in 1819 in Faizabad. He joined the army, like his father, but then left it to be part of Wajid Ali Shah's colourful court in Lucknow. He also worked at the iconic Naval Kishore Press as a proofreader, and later as an assembly poet for the nawabs of Tonk, Mangrol and Rampur. A pupil of Nasim Dehlvi, who was, in turn, a shagird of Momin Khan Momin, Tasleem's poetry exhibits passing shades of Momin Khan's style. He died in 1911.

of the Yamuna's resplendent shores continued to glaze the eyes of Dehli-wallahs with a warm patina. And Dehli, the penurious region ('ujda dayaar', as Zafar referred to it in one of his shers) continued to attract talent, not only poets, but all kinds of artistes with proficiency in all kinds of arts and crafts. Indeed, the magnet that it was for drawing artistic talent, Dehli of the time set an awe-inspiring precedent, and it's difficult to find another city like that, not just in Hindustan, but among nations of the entire world.

The seasons don't always stay the same colour. In the aftermath of 1857, Dehli's core of talent began to give way. A few were claimed by the hand of death; others scattered in different directions amidst a panicked storm of pleas for patronage to other kings and princes. People stayed on wherever they received the support they sought. Dehli became pauperised, and in turn, Hyderabad and Rampur came to be enriched. There were those that quit their life and world in Dehli in the hope that they would return; sadly though, they were never able to set eyes on their beloved city again. Those that are left in Dehli are all unsettled, sitting packed and ready to leave. Some have risen, some are rising to go, and soon, there will come a time when nobody will be left to point out where Momin, the great poet of Dehli, lived. For instance, there's hardly anybody in the city today, besides me, who knows where Momin's grave lies.

I saw these extinguishing lamps and their final impassioned efforts at a dying dawn-time refulgence. My idea took wing also from Momin's image. I felt deeply moved to light a lamp for Urdu from these poets' lights, to be able to illuminate this age for coming generations. I felt that future Urdu lovers should catch a glimpse of these last titans far from their time, however hazy it might be. People with an intellectual affinity know and understand that to be able to visualise the dead poets' faces and expressions as they recited their verses, their movements of hands and eyes, the delightful lyrical cadences, dramatic pauses, the play in their reciting voices, or how they sat down and then rose from their seats, their manner and persona, and most significantly, the poets' typical dress and style—all have the power to create a deep imaginative space of enchantment, and enhance their reading experience twice over. Without the reader having some means of delving into the writer's mind-world, to read his or her work is no more engrossing or effective than listening to an impersonal gramophone record. This is the reason why no book in today's civilised world is published without an author's prefatory note or introduction, describing the events and circumstances woven into his life when he arranged and bound his thoughts and experiences within the confines of his work's printed leaves. These are a few thoughts that have compelled me to write a couple of explanatory pages.

In this album, the reader will find many pictures that have been painted by the hands of other writers, word-images created by earlier painters. They will also find word-portraits that I have composed from photographs or other text vignettes. Mostly, I have reconstructed descriptions of persons based on actual conversations I had with older people who lived during the period, or had known such persons. Whatever the modus operandi of gathering materials to be able to recreate the mushaira in these pages, I have tried to corroborate everything and keep it authentic. And if during the course of my research, I found even the smallest contrary evidence for any event, I discarded it.

If I had found the depictions of all poets in a single place, then their military-like uniformity would have made this work eminently boring. Fortunately, it was not so. I found Azad's *Nairang-e khayaal* which sowed the idea of a mushaira in my mind, and almost immediately, by divine design, I found Karimuddin Magfoor's tazkirah, *Tab'qat-e shora-e Hind*, in whose fourth part there is a mention of a mushaira held in 1261 AH, in the month of Rajab.

I brought the two together and birthed a literary creation. There was the final matter of mixing and blending the right colours—I have taken that into my own hands. Whether the results have been good or not, I cannot tell.

As a chronicler, I could have written about the mushaira in 1261 AH (1845) as if I witnessed it all with my own eyes.

hamcho sabza baarhaa roeeda am
haft sad haftaad qaalib deeda am[28]

Like grass, I spring up again and again
Seven hundred and seventy times I am born, again and again.

I could have ensconced myself right in it, and been 'Mirza saheb'. My conscience, however, did not allow me to take credit for Karimuddin's success. Like tossing out a fly from a glass of milk, I could not distance him from the event he had played a key role in organising, and at whose home the mushaira was actually held. Indeed, he was the heart and soul of it. The only thing is, the mehfil he had organised was limited to a few select poets, and I have taken the latitude to open the door wider and admit other poets, so that almost all the prominent poets of the time have found a seat at the mushaira.

Whether I have achieved success in what I set out to do or not, only the generous reader can tell. If yes, then it's my good fortune, my hard work has paid off. If, on the other hand, I haven't achieved my objective, then at least my effort might be applauded as 'Mirza saheb set the stage for a good thing even if he wasn't quite able to sustain it, what he couldn't do, we can

[28]This is a verse by Jalaluddin Rumi (1207–1273 CE), the greatest of Sufi mystics and poets in the Persian language, originally from Khorasan, Iran. Rumi's spiritual and literary legacy transcends geographies, and to this day, translations of his works continue to be read and appreciated all over the world. His *Masnavi-ye Ma'navi* is regarded as a bestseller in the United States.

take forward.' It's possible a later writer making acquaintance with this work, and endowed with a brilliance of language and skill, might successfully take the next step and bring to life an inspiring account of those legendary poets lying asleep in the dust of time, a portrait fit to be the centrepiece of an impressive bazm-e-Urdu.

So now, I present myself in the guise of Maulvi Karimuddin saheb. And since I have dedicated all my efforts to him, I would urge my readers to address all their comments on the hits-and-misses of this work not to me, but to Maulvi Karimuddin, and as fulsomely as their hearts desire. I'm satisfied (with my effort) as is the Almighty!

Va-as-salaam!
Mirza Farhatullah Baig

Idea for a mushaira

havas ko hai nashaat-e kaar kya kya
na ho marnaa to jiine ka mazaa kya

Lust has the urge to do many, many things
If they could all be completed, life would become uninteresting.

My name is Karimuddin, I belong to Panipat. This is a hamlet about 40 kos[29] from Dehli, towards the north-west and is historically famous for its battles.[30] We were a family of maulvis, leading a comfortable life. But the wheel of fortune turned, pounded us and our days became marked by penury and want. Our property was confiscated. My grandfather sought comfort in a masjid and spent all his time in prayer. When the inquiry began for the forfeited property, importunate faith took hold of him and he did not move a finger. As a result,

---

[29]Kos is a unit of distance equal to about two miles.

[30]Three historic battles took place at Panipat. The first battle, fought in 1526 CE between Babur and Ibrahim Lodi, marked the end of the Delhi Sultanate and laid the foundation of the Mughal empire in India. The second battle took place in 1556 CE between Hemu and Akbar. It gave the Mughals a decisive victory and firmly established Akbar on the throne of Delhi. The third battle, considered to be one of the most eventful wars in eighteenth-century India, was fought in 1761 CE between the Marathas and the massive invading Afghan coalition under Ahmad Shah Abdali. The Afghans emerged victorious, while the Marathas suffered heavy losses.

we lost everything and were reduced to a state of irrevocable destitution. My father Sirajuddin, undoubtedly due to regret and shame, remained wedded to religion right until his death. I was born in 1237 AH (AD 1821) exactly on the day of Eid-ul Fitr.[31] I got my education from these very elders, but ultimately, I left Panipat because of my family's circumstances and my own restless temperament. The Dehli of my time was a self-confident city taking pride in its dominant cultural position, every mile of it bursting with experts of various arts and crafts, every direction overflowing with fountains of knowledge. As the saying goes, 'the mullah goes no further than the masjid,' so too, I left Panipat with my eyes fixed on the bright lights of Dehli.[32]

Printing presses had recently begun operating in the city,[33] and I found work as a calligraphist. After a full day's work, I would still make the time to indulge my love for knowledge and would find my way to cultural gatherings where men of letters gathered and exchanged ideas. This was also the period when Dehli College had acquired a new and modern outlook,[34] and was

[31]Eid-ul Fitr is an auspicious festive day that comes after thirty days of Ramzaan (or Ramadan) in the ninth month of the Islamic calendar.

[32]In medieval times, Delhi grew into a global hub that reached its zenith under Alauddin Khilji. Amir Khusrau, with his characteristic flourish, declared that a diamond lay hidden underneath every stone in this city that boasted of scholars who were well versed in every branch of Islamic learning, philosophy, logic and religion, a city that attracted creative talent from all over the civilised world. According to Zia-ud Din Barani, Delhi had scholars of great calibre whose equals were not to be found even in Bukhara, Samarkand, Baghdad and Egypt.
K.A. Nizami trans. Ather Farouqui, *Delhi in Historical Perspectives*, pp. 17–19.

[33]The first lithographic press was bought in 1834 by the prominent and well-connected Maulvi Muhammad Baqir, father of Muhammad Husain Azad. In 1836-37, he established the *Dehli Urdu Akhbar*. Baqir's newspaper was a mirror for Delhi's travails through the high-voltage summer months of 1857.

[34]The Delhi College (what we know as Zakir Hussain College today) was remodelled by the EIC in 1828 to provide, in addition to Oriental Studies, an education in

encouraging students to enrol. At eighteen years of age, I also enrolled at the college. My enrolment brought me some financial relief too—a scholarship of sixteen rupees. And in this way, I was able to quench my thirst for knowledge to an extent. Then again, this wasn't a time when knowledge was gained for the sheer joy of it since time was also needed for earning a livelihood. So, I got together with some friends and set up a small printing press. We rented Begum Mubarak al-nisa's haveli at Hauz Qazi and began by printing translations of famous Arabic books. The printing press did not quite yield its worth though. This was an era when Urdu poetry was at its peak—right from the Mughal Badshah to the faqir on the dusty roadside, everyone was dyed and revelling in its fresh hue.[35]

That was when I had the thought that I should organise a mushaira that would bring together the various and many poets so that I could collect and print the poets' works and their biographies. I was hopeful that printing a book on such a subject would be able to give the much-needed fillip to my languishing press. To be honest, I never had any inclination towards poetry, nor do I now. On the other hand, in my view, shairi, or writing poetry, is a decidedly unsuitable activity for people with education. It is for people of means and those with no worry about their livelihood, people with time on their hands. Such people can afford to indulge in shairi and its poetic acrobatics to please their

---

English language and literature. Then in May 1857, it was ruinously looted by the rebel soldiers, who destroyed invaluable copies of Persian and English books and manuscripts, priceless portraits, and who didn't even spare scientific instruments and chemicals. The college was kept shut by the British until 1864, when it opened with an increased focus on English at the expense of Urdu. It shut down yet again in 1877.

[35]In 1803, the Quran was translated for the first time from Persian to Urdu. This was a big milestone—an assertion of Urdu as a mature and credible language, enough to replace Persian as the *de jure lingua franca* of the Mughal court.

vanity and fill their hours.

I'm educated; so was my father and his father. I normally wouldn't give any attention at all to the wasteful activity of shairi, but necessity prevailed and I seriously pondered the idea of a mushaira. Of course, there were several issues with that as I thought about it. First, in this city, the citizens had precious little consideration for those in need, and even less so if the needy happened to be from out of town. Second, I did have some acquaintances in the city, but expectedly, they were all maulvis, and of what possible help could they be in *this* venture?

Thus wrapped up in thought, the name of Nawab Zain ul-Abidin Khan Arif came to my mind. I had met him a couple of times—a pleasant and good-natured man. He has a haveli near Lal Kuan, which is also a madrasa. He lives there. About thirty years old, he is tall, fair complexioned and impeccably attired. He has a beard, not full or thick, just a few whiskers on his chin. He is Mirza Ghalib's nephew and also his shagird.[36] For a while, he was also Shah Nasir's pupil.[37] In any case, his eminence, his affection for me and most importantly, his influence, drove me to seek his guidance and help for the idea brewing in my mind. And so, early in the morning one day, I reached his house. I was told that he had gone to meet Hakim Ahsanullah Khan,

---

[36]Ghalib loved Arif like a son, and after the untimely death of both Arif and his wife in 1852, apparently due to tuberculosis, Ghalib took on the responsibility of raising their two young sons. They stayed with Ghalib and his wife until Ghalib's death on 15 February 1869. Pavan K. Varma, *Ghalib: The Man, the Times*, p. 100.

[37]Shah Nasiruddin 'Nasir' (1756–1838 CE) was Bahadur Shah Zafar's first ustad. His family called him miyaan Kallu because of his dark complexion. His poetry earned him recognition at the court of Shah Alam (Bahadur Shah's grandfather) and also gave him the gift of travel, taking him as far south as Hyderabad, and east to Lucknow. He travelled to the Deccan three times, and the fourth time when he went there, he did not come back to Delhi. Shah Nasir is buried in the khanqah of Qazi Makhdum Musa in Hyderabad. Azad, *Aab-e hayat*, Part 4. *https://dsal.uchicago.edu/books/PK2155.H8413/387404d5.html*

Wazir-e-azam, who lived close by in Sirkiwalan. When I came by again after some time and asked at the door, I was informed that Nawab Zain ul-Abidin Khan had returned and was indoors. The chobdaar relayed the information of my arrival, and I was sent for.

It is a large and splendid house. There is a fountain in the courtyard, the courtyard leading up to a large raised verandah in the front, that in turn opens into spacious double halls. The house is remarkably well done up; everything spells class. I saw Nawab saheb sitting there, leaning back against gao-takiyas. But what was this? I couldn't recognise him. He was looking thin as a stick and his face had sprouted wrinkles. I greeted him with a customary salaam and asked after his health and well-being.

With a despondent air, he replied, 'Maulvi saheb, what should I say? I get this sinking feeling. There doesn't seem to be any specific ailment with manifest symptoms, and I'm getting treated, but there seems to be no improvement. It's now time to move on. I'm enjoying earthly delights for just a little while longer. But you tell me, what brings you here?'

I narrated to him the situation with my newly acquired press, its prospects and my idea of a mushaira for the poets of the city. I also explained how I needed his help. He listened and thought silently for a few moments. Then with a deep sigh, he said, 'Miyaan Karimuddin! You have indeed struck upon a good idea. However, its execution presents some difficulties. You have no idea how previous mushairas in Dehli have given rise to differences amongst people, created a rift even between friends. In fact, before I die, I too want to attend one last great mushaira where the city's best and most refined poets are present. But somehow, I feel doubtful about it. You keep trying, I will too; it's possible we might be able to pull it off. Wait, let Hakim saheb come in—' he broke off and turned to instruct the chobdaar accordingly.

'I just thought of a plan,' he said to me, 'if it works, then my last wish shall be fulfilled and your mission too will be accomplished.'

We were talking about this when Hakim Ahsanullah Khan entered.[38] Fair-skinned, a full white beard on a round face with scattered pockmarks, his eyes seemed to overflow with intelligence. He was dressed in white attire from head to toe. Hakim saheb is an expert in medicine and also highly knowledgeable about history. I greeted him with a respectful aadaab and he smiled in gracious acknowledgement. Then turning to Nawab saheb, he prompted, 'Aapki taariif, his introduction?'[39]

Nawab saheb obliged. 'He's one of my old friends; doesn't himself write poetry, but he has a good understanding of it. Nowadays, he's toying with the idea of penning a tazkirah of the poets of Dehli, complete with a portrait of their physical appearance and a selection of their kalaam. He had come to take my advice; as you know, I love these things. Now as my end draws near, it's my heartfelt wish to partake in an old-style mushaira. If you could help, then our difficulties could be eased.'

Hakim saheb countered, 'Miyaan Arif, for God's sake, don't speak so despairingly. You are young, and inshallah, you will soon get better! And what exactly is your ailment? Only your imagination! But tell me, what sort of help do you need from me?'

Nawab saheb explained, 'Hakimji, simply this, if you could help Karimuddin reach Badshah Jahanpanah.' He added, 'I would go myself, but I am in no condition for that. I will explain everything to him, how to conduct himself and other formalities.

---

[38]Hakim Ahsanullah Khan was Bahadur Shah Zafar's prime minister and confidant. He was also a close friend of the poet Mirza Ghalib. His house was burnt down in August 1857 by incensed rebel troops who accused the hakim of treason. It greatly saddened Ghalib; thankfully though, Hakim saheb's life was spared.

[39]The Urdu phrase 'aapki taariif' has no true equivalent in English. At best, it can be translated as introducing a person to someone with a gracious presentation of their best and praiseworthy qualities.

If Hazrat Zillullah[40] agrees to send his ghazal then there won't be any difficulty in arranging the mushaira. If, unfortunately, he is not agreeable to it, then it will become clear that the thought of organising a mushaira is futile. Now, about making various arrangements for it, I will take care of all that myself. What does this poor man (Karimuddin) know about these things?'

Hakim saheb thought for some time and then responded, 'Arif, I'm prepared to do all this for you. Even more so, to distract your mind. With this keeping you busy for a few weeks, hopefully you will get over your phantom ailment. I won't take it up with Badshah Salamat, but I will introduce your friend here to Saheb-e-alam Mirza Fath-ul-mulk Bahadur.[41] He is fired up these days for a mushaira. He has spoken to Huzoor about it a couple of times, but the latter has been putting it off. If your friend can convince Saheb-e-alam, then I'm sure the latter will cajole Badshah Salamat into giving his consent.'

Turning to me, he said, 'Come tomorrow at 1 p.m. to the Qila Mu'alla, Maulvi saheb. I will tell the chobdaar to bring you inside. After that, it's all up to you and your fate!'

Hakim saheb called Khuda Bakhsh and told him, 'Tomorrow, Maulvi saheb will come to the haveli at 1 p.m.[42] Bring him to my

---

[40]Hazrat Zillullah or Shadow of God was a title for the Mughal Badshah. Other forms of address included Badshah Salamat, Badshah Jahanpanah, Pir-o-murshid, Huzoor-e-wala or simply Huzoor.

[41]Baig's original footnote: His name was Mirza Fakhruddin, title, Mirza Fath-ul-mulk Shah Bahadur, aka Mirza Fakhru, pen name (takhallus) 'Ramz'. He was Zafar's second son and was crowned 'Wali Ahad' after his older brother Mirza Mumammad Dara Bakht, aka Mirza Shabbo 'Wali Ahad' died in 1849. But Mirza Fakhru died in 1856 at the age of forty. After his death, Mirza Jawan Bakht's ascension was doomed from the start, and after the 1857 Uprising, the claim of the Mughal lineage to the throne ceased entirely.

[42]Baig's original footnote: Qila-e-Dehli was also popularly known as 'Lal haveli' or only 'haveli'.

baithak.' Thereafter, Hakim saheb returned to his conversation with Nawab saheb, and I took their leave with an aadaab and headed home.

Next day, around 1 p.m., I reached the Qila Mu'alla, dressed in my maulvi best—a long formal tunic and turban. I saw Khuda Bakhsh, the chobdaar, waiting outside Lahori Darwaza, and I was duly taken to Hakim saheb's baithak. This baithak used to be called nishast in the past and it adjoins the Diwaan-e Aam.

Hakim saheb sat there at his desk, writing something. When he saw me, he cheerfully exclaimed, 'Oh Maulvi saheb! I have done your work! This morning itself I met Saheb-e-alam Mirza Fath-ul-mulk Bahadur and brought up your idea of a mushaira. He was delighted and immediately said, "I will take permission from Jahanpanah. But the arrangements should be properly appropriate, keeping in mind that we will be present." Do sit though. Possibly, you will be summoned for an audience.'

I sat down to one side and almost instantly, the chobdaar came in and announced, 'Who is Karimuddin? Huzoor-e-wala wishes to see him!'

I immediately broke into a sweat. I'd thought I would come and meet Hakim saheb, and everything would somehow get automatically handled. But no, that was not to be! What was this about an audience with Jahanpanah, and that too at such an inconvenient time, when all the air had been sucked out of my lungs?

Well, if the doctor has ordered immediate death, so be it!

I rose from my chair and silently walked behind the chobdaar with my head lowered as he led the way inside the Qila. All along the route, in an attempt to calm my turbulent mind and racing pulse, I silently recited the Ayat al-Kursi.[43] Not once did

[43]Ayat al-Kursi is regarded by Muslims as one of the most powerful ayahs of the Quran because when it is recited, the greatness of the Almighty is confirmed. A person who recites it is in God's protection.

I raise my head to see where this 'Khuda', this God was taking me. The Qila Mu'alla had always fascinated me and I had a great curiosity to view its grandeur from up close. I now had the chance, but not the eyes. My nervousness at the thought of a royal audience had killed all my curiosity. We kept walking, the chobdaar and I, and after some time, my eyes were covered with a shimmering haze. Finally, and only with God's mercy, we arrived near the steps of the Diwaan-e Khaas. The chobdaar made me stand there while he went inside to announce me.

Hazrat Jahanpanah was, at that time, gracing the royal hammam. Those who have not seen Dehli's Qila may not be able to appreciate the pure pleasure of being seated in the hammam during the summers. What is the hammam actually? It is a magnificently architected building with two large chambers or sections, one warm and the other cool. The part of the building that is in the direction of the Moti Masjid is the warm chamber, and the other chamber, facing the River Yamuna, is the cool one. Thick dampened khas screens, made of hay, are lowered over the arcades of the chamber to turn it into a cool and fragrant khas khaana.[44] The large chamber has a canal running through its entire length and in the centre are several large gurgling fountains. So, what is the hammam? It is a little piece of heaven![45]

I waited by the steps for whatever was supposed to come next. There was no sign of the chobdaar. He'd been gone a long time, I thought. Standing there in the harsh afternoon sunlight, I felt

---

[44]Thick porous screens of khas (or khas-khas), continuously dampened with scented water, are hung on the windward facing entrances so that the hot loo winds are cooled by evaporation into a refreshing breeze, and the chamber remains fragrant and airy.

[45]The hammam, with its ornamental ponds and walls embellished with fine trelliswork, was an exclusive place for the Badshah to grant audience, on rare occasions, to the most favoured or honoured persons. He also used it for prayer and meditation, and for uninterrupted rest and respite.

all shrivelled up. Drenched in sweat, my neck bent, drops of sweat dripping rhythmically from my nose, the thought crossed my mind that perhaps, I should just turn back. But then, sanity returned. To run away after being summoned for an audience was rude and unbecoming, and second, since I hadn't paid any attention on my way here, how would I know my way back?

Mercifully, this problem also met with its solution even as I mulled over my fate. The chobdaar came back. 'Chaliye!' he announced. This simple utterance produced the most extraordinary effect—quite by themselves my legs began to shake like jelly and my heart began to tremble. Somehow cajoling my jelly-feet to move, stepping clumsily here and there, I managed to step inside the royal hammam.

The chobdaar called out, 'Proceed with reverence, you are in the presence of Hazrat Jahanpanah Salamat, may he live long and prosper. You may now do your salutations!'

Nawab Zain ul-Abidin Khan had instructed me on this part and I had learnt it well. I bowed deeply, almost to the ground, and reverentially offered seven salutations. Then I presented the nazr to Jahanpanah. At some point during these courtesies, my eyes strayed from the floor and I caught a glimpse of the surroundings. Our revered saint and guide, Hazrat Pir-o-murshid[46] was ensconced on a small silver bed, and by his side on the edge of the bed sat Mirza Fakhru, pressing his feet.

Who in Dehli has not had the fortune of setting eyes on Hazrat Zillullah? And here he was, right before my eyes. Of medium height and spare build, in his markedly oblong-shaped face lay luminous brooding eyes and an aquiline nose. He had a dark, wheatish complexion, a long neck, prominent cheekbones and a wide jaw. His head was shaven. On his upper lip sat a

[46]The convention of referring to the Emperor as Pir-o-murshid (mentor and guide) was established during Shahjahan's time. In Bahadur Shah Zafar's case, he was a practicing Sufi and formally accepted pupils or murids.

trimmed moustache. I noticed his threadlike white beard, thin on the cheeks and with a little more volume on the chin. The gossamer lines on his face gave away his seventy years vintage. His hair was quite white, but in his beard a few dark strands were still to be seen. Despite his advanced years and obvious frailty, his voice came crisp and strong. He was dressed in a single-width green-coloured, gold-embroidered silk pyjama and a fine white Dhaka muslin kurta.[47] In front of him was a low stool on which lay a jaamavaar[48] khaftaan and his embroidered chau-goshia.

And then there was Mirza Fakhru. He was the reflection of his father in a mirror. About thirty-two or thirty-three years old, he was different from his father only in his youth. Whereas the Emperor's skin had the darker tinge of dotage, Mirza Fakhru had a ruddy wheatish complexion. The Emperor's beard was completely white, while Mirza Fakhru sported a dark beard. As I saw it, one badshah was lying on the cot and another was sitting beside him. Both gave me a long look. Then Badshah Salamat spoke, 'Amaan,[49] are you the one named Karimuddin? You seem

---

[47]Dhaka muslin was introduced to the Mughals by Nur Jahan, Jahangir's powerful queen of Persian origin and an aesthete with a keen eye for fine textiles and delicate embroidery. She cultivated special workshops in Dhaka to produce the finest muslin, called 'mulmul kas', for the Mughal court. Under her patronage, Dhaka muslins and their exquisite designs (some of which were created by Nur Jahan herself, like the dudami or flowered muslins) acquired great fame and were considered high fashion for centuries. *Indian Horizons*, Vol. 63, No. 2, April–June 2016.

[48]Jaamavaar is a flowered silk fabric that was favoured by both men and women.

[49]The term 'amaan' (with a nasalised 'maa') is a contraction of two words—'ay' and 'miyaan'. It is a friendly and informal form of address, quite like the word 'hey' in English. It continues to be in use in Urdu-speaking regions even today. Baig's original footnote: Towards the end of the time of Qila-e-mu'alla and its ethos, the princes and nobility would often address both men and women with 'amaan'. This form of language was carried with the migrating and travelling Dehli poets to Hyderabad in the late nineteenth century, and is therefore, also common in the everyday spoken tongue in Hyderabad to this day.

to be from somewhere outside Dehli...'

With the greatest politeness, I replied. 'Indeed sire, your servant is from Panipat. However, he has been in the shade of your benevolence and kindness since childhood.'

Badshah Salamat continued, 'Amaan, Mirza Fakhru was just talking about you. I would myself like to have a mushaira in the Diwaan-e Aam, as it used to be in the old days, but what can I do? The winds are so adverse, it does not seem appropriate. It's true that they are the enemy, but still, may the Almighty keep them safe, what good is such enmity that it doesn't permit a few moments of sitting together in friendship? When we used to have the mushaira in the Diwaan-e Aam, it went well for a while. Then slowly, I sensed a dying of enthusiasm among the people and so I stopped having it. Munshi Faiz Parsa started a mushaira in the madrasa of Ghaziuddin Khan, outside Ajmeri Darwaza,[50] but soon enough, it also scattered like twigs. In the end, it was a good thing the rhyme ended in "tiliyaan" (twigs). If, God forbid, the rhyme had ended with "lakdiyaan" (logs) instead, who knows how many people's heads would have been hurt.[51] You are planning to have a mushaira, but how will you

---

[50]The Ghaziuddin Madrasa was built in the late seventeenth century by Ghaziuddin Khan, a nobleman during Aurangzeb's reign. In 1825, it came to house the Delhi College.

[51]Munshi Faiz Parsa was a teacher in Delhi College and in eternal competition with Shah Nasir, the Badshah's earlier teacher. In his passion for poetry, Munshi Parsa instituted a mushaira in the school and declared it as being crucial for the progress of Urdu literature. On the day of the mushaira, he obtained special permission for the city gates to stay open beyond the usual hour of 9 p.m., all the way until 2 a.m.

The best-known poets and nobles of the city attended the mushaira, and all eyes were on Shah Nasir and Munshi Parsa. Shah Nasir recited a ghazal with '*qafas ki tiliyaan, khas ki tiliyaan*'. In a later assembly of the mushaira, the intense competition between the two caused a serious confrontation, and eventually, the mushaira had to be discontinued. For more, see Frances W. Pritchett, *Nets of Awareness: Urdu Poetry and its Critics*, p. 73.

handle the clashing of the elephants? Ustad Zauq is reserved in his speech and mostly stays silent, but God save you from Hafiz Veeraan. He's sure to get into an argument. And as you know, when a blind man strikes, there's nothing one can do![52] If someone is even slightly critical of Ustad Zauq, Veeraan will immediately react and it will be difficult to control him. Miyaan, I don't see you being equal to this mammoth task.'

I humbly conceded, 'Qibla-e-alam, indeed it's a tall order and I accept I'm not equal to the task. But it is Nawab Zain ul-Abidin Khan Arif who has taken on the responsibility of making all the various arrangements for the mushaira.'

That seemed to put the Emperor at ease. 'Then I'm assured. He's intelligent and sensible, and quite capable of managing both Mirza Nausha and Momin Khan. As for Ustad Zauq, I will tell him of your endeavour. God willing, the mushaira will take place as you have planned. But I'm telling you, you should go and meet these people beforehand to ensure they don't let you down in the end. I will not be able to come, neither will Mirza Shabbo. But Mirza Fakhru will go in my place, and inshallah, I will also send my ghazal with him. Tell me, what is the tarah you have assigned for the mushaira? It is the tarah that is at the root of disagreements; you should give enough thought and consideration before assigning a tarah.'

As he was speaking, an annoyed voice floated out from an adjoining chamber. 'Ai hey! What a be-tarah manner for the

---

[52]Hafiz Ghulam Rasool Veeraan was a pupil of Ustad Zauq. The sightless Veeraan was known to have a peevish attitude, and that is what Badshah Zafar is referring to. His choice of the Urdu phrase '*andhe kii daad na faryaad, andha maar baithega*' harks to an outdoor game in which a blindfolded person wields a stick and chants, '*Andhe kii daad na faryaad, andha maar baithega*'. Others involved in the game make a playful din until one of them is struck by the blindfolded person's stick. And so the game goes.

maid to put the child to sleep!'[53]

The moment he heard the exclamation, Badshah Salamat excitedly proclaimed, 'There you go! Here's the faal-e-gosh, the overheard cue.[54] For this mushaira, you shall give no tarah at all. Whatever metre, whichever rhyme, whatever radiif or qafiya, let each person recite as he wishes.[55] You have nothing to gain or lose!'

And that was that.

My next concern was when it should be held. 'Pir-o-murshid! What date would you advise for it?'

Badshah Salamat replied, 'Set it for 14 Rajab. It's a good day, a full moon night.[56] Today is the fifth, so you have all of nine days. A lot of arrangements can be made within this time. As per the Roman calendar, it will be the twentieth of July. The weather will also cool down by then.' After a brief pause, he concluded, 'All right then, Khuda hafiz!'

I bowed, expressed a prayer for Badshah Salamat's long life and prosperity, and took my leave, feeling pleased. As per protocol, I began to walk backward, in reverse step. Mirza Fakhru[57] had not

---

[53]The implication is that the maid has put the child to sleep willy-nilly, in a disorderly or improper manner.

[54]A faal-e-gosh is a prediction or a cue taken from the first words to reach the listeners' ears, as when overheard from passers-by.

[55]The tarah is a metred rhyme that is given as an example to fix the metre, qafiya and radiif for the ghazals to be recited in a tarahi mushaira. In this instance, the Badshah has done away with the tarah, and so gone against convention in his not entirely unknown whimsical fashion.

[56]Zafar surrounded himself with Hindu astrologers and consulted them all the time for timing events and taking advantage of auspicious days.

[57]Mirza Fakhru was highly accomplished like other princes of that age. He had mastery over many calligraphic styles and was also an expert rider and archer. He held the rank of supreme master in music and dance, and also composed poetry in rekhta. Although he did not compose in Persian, he remained an avid student of Persian prose and poetry under Maulana Sehbai's tutorship. He also knew English

interrupted the Emperor even once, but I knew he had done the real work behind the scenes. Why else would the exalted Badshah bestow this favour upon an ordinary person like me? It is indeed true that when the Almighty is merciful, things turn out right.

I now felt that my audience with the Emperor had not been as difficult as this final exit from His Majesty's presence, this walking backwards. My feet had barely touched the ground and walked two-three backward steps when I banged into a wall behind me. Scarcely had I collected my wits after this collision when my foot mysteriously landed in the canal. Finally, after a thousand mishaps, I emerged outside and almost instantly the chobdaar appeared at my side. I gave him some money in acknowledgement of his services, let him go and then proceeded to meet Hakim saheb. Hakim saheb was there, waiting for me. After I had related my experience, he explained. 'Maulvi saheb, it's like this: Mirza Fakhru had been getting restless for many days, he's been wanting to have a mushaira for some time now. It's all his handiwork, otherwise would it have been this simple a matter to decide? But I'm relieved your wish has been granted. You should go and inform miyaan Arif too, he will be waiting for you at my house.'

I reached Hakim saheb's house and indeed, Nawab Arif was there, awaiting my arrival and what news I would bring. I told him the whole story and he exclaimed in relief, 'Good! Now that this problem has been resolved, you should go to the houses of Ustad Zauq, Mirza Nausha and Hakim Momin Khan. But mind you, you'll need to be careful; all three are very conscious of their stature and expect a certain conduct befitting that. If they perceive even the slightest lapse in your conversation or manner, it will

---

reasonably well. Unlike other princes who confined themselves to the Qila, Mirza Fakhru occasionally rode into the city and had friendly relations with distinguished Indians and British officers.

Shamsur Rahman Faruqi, *The Mirror of Beauty*, p. 805.

ruin everything. Should you find any of them being particularly difficult, feel free to use my name and our connection. Who knows, that might do the trick and they might come around. The second thing is, in two days' time, I want you to vacate the haveli of Begum Mubarak al-nisa,[58] where you have your printing press, and hand it over to me. That's the place where I would like to organise the mushaira and have the seating arrangement.'

A little perplexed, I asked, 'And then where will I go?'

He assuaged my worry. 'Come to my house for eight nine days. No doubt, it would be bothersome for you, but nothing can be done. When we are inviting the princes from the Qila, we need to choose a suitable venue and make the right arrangements in every way. What remains to be seen is how much it will cost to do all this.'

'How much would a mushaira cost? Why, at the most, a hundred to a hundred and twenty-five rupees,' I confidently said.

Nawab saheb smiled. 'Miyaan Karimuddin, what do you know of the expenses that are incurred in such mushairas? Even if we spend a thousand to two thousand rupees, we should count ourselves lucky to be let off cheaply!'

I was struck dumb when I heard this. 'Nawab saheb, that much? If so, my salaam to such a mushaira from a safe distance! I will never be able to raise this kind of money even if I were to sell my printing press and my very own self.'

'You stay out of this matter of money and expenses,' he

---

[58]Begum Mubarak al-nisa was the widow of Sir David Ochterlony, one of the best known 'white Mughals' in British India. Mubarak Begum, nicknamed Generallee Begum, was Ochterlony's favourite bibi (wife) and wielded substantial influence, for which she was also intensely disliked. By 1863, the begum's haveli, the venue of Farhatullah Baig's historical-fictional mushaira, had been damaged beyond recognition in a planned demolition drive on the orders of Lord Canning. Masjid Mubarak Begum still exists near Hauz Qazi, and is known as Randi ki Masjid.

William Dalrymple, *The White Mughals: Love and Betrayal in Eighteenth-century India*, p. 183.

answered gently, reassuring me. 'The Almighty will forge a way out of this difficulty too. And then, why are you anxious? I have taken on the responsibility for this, so just leave it to me. You simply sit and watch the tamasha.'

After a pause, he continued, 'But I will require you to vacate your house tomorrow. Only nine days are left and there's a lot to be done. Now, Khuda hafiz! You should go and get some rest, you must be tired. Tomorrow morning, you should give priority to two things—make preparations to get your things together and vacate your house. Then make a round of the three ustads' homes. Be sure to inform me when you vacate your house. And of course, please come to my house with all your belongings, there's no need to feel shy about it. After all, you are vacating your house because of me.'

It had been a long and eventful day, and I returned home tired. By the time I packed my press and put together my things, the day had ended and my mind was full of thoughts and plans for the next day. Next morning, I had my personal things sent to Nawab Zain ul-Abidin Khan's house, and I myself turned towards Kabuli Darwaza[59] to start my obeisance of the ustads with the venerable Ustad Zauq.[60]

Ustad Zauq lives near the Kabuli Darwaza in a humble house with a small doorway but having a narrow space on one side of it. The courtyard within is small, so small that if two cots were to be laid out, there'd be very little space for movement. In the front is a modest-sized hall and right above it, a small room. From the courtyard, a passageway leads to the zenana within.

---

[59]After September 1857, Kabuli Darwaza came to be called Khuuni Darwaza; it remains so to this day. It is an archway where William Hodson shot dead the three Mughal princes—Mirza Mughal, Khizr Sultan and Abu Bakr—in cold blood, at point-blank range, for actively aiding the rebels during the Uprising.

[60]Please read Sheikh Mohammad Ibrahim Zauq's brief biographical sketch in *Appendix B*.

When I reached his house, Ustad Zauq was sitting in his courtyard on a cot made of woven rope, and smoking his huqqa. On another similar cot sat his favourite shagird, Hafiz Ghulam Rasool Veeraan. He is sightless, and I remembered that he was the one Hazrat Jahanpanah had warned me to be careful of. Ustad Zauq is of medium height and build, with a warm wheatish complexion and pockmarks on his face. His features stand out prominently with his large, bright eyes and intense gaze. That morning, he was dressed in a narrow-bottomed white pyjama with a white kurta and a matching white angrakha. On his head, he wore a round white muslin cap.

I stepped into the courtyard and the sound of my footsteps startled Hafiz Veeraan. He asked, 'Kaun hai, who's there?'

I gave my name and added that I had come to pay my respects to Ustad Zauq. As soon as he heard this, Ustad Zauq invited me in with the utmost courtesy. 'Come in, please come in.'

I greeted him respectfully. 'Aadaab!' he responded. 'Sit down, do take a seat.'

I went and sat beside Hafiz Veeraan on the cot. In an easy and pleasant manner, Ustad Zauq asked me what brought me to his house. I explained that I was planning to have a mushaira at Hauz Qazi, for which the date had been fixed for 14 Rajab. With a formality befitting the master's standing, I concluded, 'If huzoor would be so gracious as to honour this humble servant with his presence, it would be a great kindness indeed.'

I had barely finished speaking when Hafiz Veeraan got agitated and retorted, 'Go away, go away! From where did this mushaira appear? Ustad has no time for it. Why don't you go to the "adopted" Mirza[61] instead of troubling the Ustad?'

---

[61]Baig's original footnote: In those days, there was a strong rumour in Dehli that Mirza Nausha (Ghalib) was not actually Mirza Abdullah Baig's son, that the latter had only brought him up, and in reality, Ghalib was the child of a Kashmiri. Hafiz Veeraan alludes to this.

Ustad Zauq admonished him as he would a child. 'Bhai Hafiz Veeraan! You don't stop speaking! Just like that, you get into an argument with everybody in the world.'

Hafiz Veeraan persisted, 'Ustad! If they speak badly to you, why should we sit quietly? They say one thing, we will give back a hundred times over. Look now, miyaan Ashufta is having his day—only yesterday he referred to you as a barber.[62] But I took him to task, such that he'll remember it all his life. I taught him a firm lesson, not just him but seven generations after him too.'

Ustad Zauq laughed and answered calmly, 'No, my friend! Why do you court trouble for my sake? Everyone can call me whatever they wish. I will respond to them all with this rubai:

tu bhalaa hai to buraa ho nahiiN saktaa ai Zauq
hai buraa voh hi ke jo tujh ko buraa jaantaa hai

aur jo KHud tu hi buraa hai to voh sach kahta hai
kyuN buraa kehne se uske tu buraa maantaa hai

If you are good, O Zauq, you cannot be bad
He who thinks you are bad is himself bad

And if indeed you are bad, he tells the truth
Then why feel bad when he claims you are bad.'

I informed him of my audience with the Badshah the previous day, and that Zillullah had given his blessings to the mushaira and kindly consented to send Mirza Fath-ul-mulk Bahadur in his lieu. What's more, he'd even agreed to send his ghazal with Mirza Fakhru to grace the mehfil. Upon hearing this, Hafiz Veeraan sat back deflated. Ustad Zauq replied, 'Yes, I remember now. Last evening, Hazrat Pir-o-murshid told me about your mushaira and

---

[62]Baig's original footnote: Everyone in Dehli used to refer to Ustad Zauq as 'barber'. It is another matter that Muhammad Husain Azad put a sword in the hand of Zauq's father and thus made Zauq a soldier's son (in *Aab-e hayat*).

urged me to attend it. I will certainly come, inshallah! But tell me, what tarah have you assigned for it?'

I narrated the be-tarah incident that had occurred at the Qila and the fact that Zille Subhani had swept aside the constraint of an assigned tarah for this mushaira. Every poet had the freedom to choose the metre, the radiif and the qafiya for his ghazal. Ustad Zauq seemed pleased with this new scheme. As I spoke, he nodded, 'Bohat khoob! Bohat khoob! Excellent! Superb!'

But I noticed that Hafiz Veeraan wasn't pleased about this departure from convention, his clouded brow was evidence. He muttered, 'God help us! Let's see what becomes of this mushaira… Hazrat Pir-o-murshid comes up with these ushqule, these strange new ideas.'[63] He kept speaking but I ignored him and took my leave after offering my salaam to Ustad Zauq.

Next in line was Asadullah Khan Ghalib. I passed through the main thoroughfare of Chandni Chowk and reached Ballimaran. Gali Kasim Jaan cuts across in front of Hakim Mahmud Khan saheb's house, and there on the left-hand side, the first house is Mirza Nausha's. It stands behind the masjid and has two entrances, one to the mardana and the other to the zenana. There is a passage leading to the mahalsara from within the mardana also. The door sill of the outer entrance is somewhat sunken below ground level. A room stands above the entrance, flanked by two smaller ante-rooms on either side that are shielded from the heat and sun. During the hot Dehli summers, Mirza saheb spends his afternoons in one of these cooler rooms. Coming in through the entrance, I find myself in a small courtyard; visible in front is a double hall.

When I reached, I found him seated in the inner hall, leaning against a gao-takiya and engrossed in writing. Mirza Nausha is

[63]Baig's original footnote: I (Farhatullah Baig) don't know which tongue this word comes from, but in Dehli, it is commonly used to mean a 'shagoofa' (something strange or new).

about fifty years old; he is good looking and tall with a broad physique. He has strong emphatic features and a beard that is full, not luxuriant. His complexion is ruddy, with a faint and attractive golden tinge.[64] His front two teeth are broken. On his bald head, he wears a tall black fur cap, resembling a kulah-e-papakh.[65] He sat there, dressed in a single-width white pyjama, a matching white muslin angrakha and a pale yellow jaamavaar choga or cloak on top.[66]

As I entered, he registered my presence and lifted his eyes even as his pen kept moving. With a bow, I wished him aadaab. Silently, he nodded a response and gestured to me to take a seat. I settled myself on one side, and just then, Nawab Ziauddin Ahmad Khan arrived. He is the brother of Nawab Aminuddin Khan of Loharu. He takes the pen name 'Rakhshaan' in Urdu and 'Nayyar' in Persian. About forty years old, he is a man of many-splendoured talents. Known to have mastery over history, geography, philosophy, the science of names, genealogy and etymology, he rounds it off with elegance in writing and interest in other fields of knowledge. Mirza Nausha is known to have great affection for him.

Short-statured, slender and fair-skinned, he has fine features and sheathed eyes, with a small well-trimmed beard on his chin. All in all, he's an extremely attractive man. Adding to this impression was his attire—a white pyjama and a matching white angrakha with a stiff four-cornered embroidered chau-goshia on his head.

---

[64]'Champai', meaning the hue of a champa flower, is the word used to describe Mirza Nausha's complexion.

Also read Mirza Ghalib's brief biographical sketch in *Appendix B*.

[65]A kulah-e-papakh is a wool hat worn by men. It is high and round and perched on the head, rather than being snugly fitted like a cap. It is commonly seen in Turkey and Uzbekistan. The word 'papakh' is of Turkic language origin.

[66]Baig's original footnote: Among all the Qila-e-Dehli personalities, Mirza Ghalib is always pictured in a certain unique way. This has been drawn from that image.

A scarf was neatly draped in a triangle over his shoulders. I rose and offered him a polite salaam. He came forward and took my hand in the traditional greeting, then sat down to one side silently and respectfully, tucking his feet beneath his thighs. In a few minutes Mirza Ghalib finished his writing work.

He turned towards Nawab saheb and exclaimed, 'Miyaan Nayyar! When did you come in?' He continued, 'This Mirza Tuftah troubles me no end. The fellow's poetic passion and his pen's flow seem endless—in each letter he encloses eight to ten ghazals for correction. I get exhausted making revisions, one after another.'[67]

Then he turned to me and said, 'I think you are Maulvi Karimuddin saheb.'

I nodded. 'Yes, indeed!'

He continued, 'Hazrat, I knew the purpose of your visit even before you entered. Yesterday, Arif Miyaan had come and made me promise that I would be present for your mushaira.' Turning to Nayyar, he asked, 'Say miyaan Nayyar, will you also come with me?'

Nayyar agreed without demur. 'Wherever you are, I am too! If you attend the mushaira, inshallah, I will happily accompany you.'

Mirza Nausha went on, 'And where is Alai till now? I've been waiting for him since yesterday. Oh! Here he comes…' To Alai, who had just entered, he exclaimed, 'Bhai, you have a long life! I was just asking about you.'

Nawab Alauddin Khan Alai is Wali Ahad of the Nawab of Loharu. He is twenty-three or twenty-four, of medium height, and has a wheatish complexion. He has a round face, prominent

[67]Here Ghalib is referring to his chief shagird, Hargopal Tuftah. The postal service had been established in the mid-nineteenth century, and Ghalib and Tuftah not only corresponded for correction of the latter's verses, but Ghalib also sent printed copies of his own poetry for distribution and reading.

Ali Khan Mahmudabad, *Poetry of Belonging: Muslim Imaginings of India*, p. 50.

features and a rich beard turned upward. His eyes are sharbati, having a reddish tinge that comes from the whites of the eyes having prominent blood vessels. He was dressed stylishly in a tapering narrow-bottomed pyjama, a white jamdani[68] angrakha and a short-sleeved black velvet upper-coat open from the front. A matching black velvet chau-goshia topped off his ensemble.

He offered his salutations, sat down on one side and then said to Mirza Ghalib, 'Indeed, I got delayed; I guessed you would be waiting for me.' He then looked towards me and asked, 'And pray, what's your introduction?'

Mirza Nausha gave an account of the planned mushaira and stated, 'Alai, you should also come with us. Hopefully you're not going to Loharu in the near future?'

He replied, 'Very good, sir. If you will go, I will also make myself available.'

Now that this matter had been settled, I withdrew, and from there I turned to Nawab Zain ul-Abidin Khan's house. He had vacated a part of the mardana for me. The things I had sent in the morning had already been unpacked and neatly arranged in the room. I freshened up, ate the food that was sent to my room and then lay down for a nap.

Around four o'clock, I awoke and quickly got ready to head out to Hakim Momin Khan's house.

Hakim saheb's house is in Chelon ka Kucha.[69] On my way

---

[68]Jamdani, a fine fabric embroidered with flowers or other motifs, was popularly used in men's and women's apparel.

[69]This is Kucha Chelan in present-day Delhi. In the aftermath of the 1857 Uprising, it faced a veritable slaughter; an estimated 1,400 people were brutally murdered. Kucha Chelan had been famous for being the most intellectual muhalla in Delhi and well-known people who were the pride of the city lived here. Zahir Dehlvi, a page in Badshah Zafar's court, and who later penned his memoirs in Hyderabad said, 'They (intellectuals of Kucha Chelan) had no parallels in their own day, nor will we ever see their like again.'
William Dalrymple, *The Last Mughal: The Fall of a Dynasty, Delhi, 1857*, p. 387.

there, I ran into Maulvi Imam Bakhsh Sehbai. He has been my teacher in Dehli College.[70] He is about forty, has a wheatish complexion and a few pockmarks here and there on his face. Of slight build, he has shoulder-length hair. When I met him, he was dressed in a single-width white pyjama, white angrakha and a long cloak with exquisite Kashmiri embroidery. A small white turban was tied around his head. He also lives in Chelon ka Kucha and was surprised to see me. He asked where I was headed. When I told him I was going to Hakim Momin Khan's house, and also what it was about, he took it upon himself to accompany me. 'Come, I'm also going there.'

Hakim Momin Khan's house is right in front of Hakim Aaga Jaan ka Chhatta.[71] It has a large and impressive entrance with a spacious courtyard within, and around this, the house rises. Two smaller courtyards can be seen on either side of this main courtyard, and in front are two capacious double halls. A room has been built above the rear hall, while the roof of the front hall has been converted into an adjoining terrace with a low parapet.[72] White floor coverings adorn the halls and a carpet is spread in the centre of the inner hall. On the carpet is seated Hakim saheb, leaning comfortably on a gao-takiya. His pupils Hakim Sakhanand Raqam and Mirza Rahimuddin Haya sit

---

[70]Maulvi Imam Bakhsh Sehbai was a reputed poet and scholar of Persian and Arabic, and to be his student was a great honour and pride. Sehbai was one of the Kucha Chelan residents who was ruthlessly murdered along with his two sons in September 1857.

[71]A neighbourhood (muhalla) in present-day Matia Mahal in Chandni Chowk.

[72]Baig's original footnote: I (Farhatullah Baig) have myself seen this house about twenty-two years ago. Three sides of the house had been levelled. The front portion was still intact. I couldn't see the reason for the low height of the upper parapet wall. Hakim Momin Khan had tripped over that parapet and fallen to the ground below, resulting in a broken arm and leg, and that ultimately led to his death. It was almost like he had made preparations for his own end!

respectfully at the edge of the carpet, their feet tucked beneath their thighs. They are both silent; like they were in a durbar where nobody has the courage to lift their gaze or speak out of turn or without a good reason.

Hakim Momin Khan must be forty years or thereabouts. He is tall and well built, with a broad chest, narrow waist and strong muscular arms. His fair complexion has a touch of a pale greenish hue. His wide brilliant eyes with long lashes and arching brows are perfectly matched by an aquiline nose, well-shaped lips tinted vermilion with paan and missi-stained teeth.[73] He sports a light moustache and a lush beard. I noticed he has long and well-shaped fingers. His hair is long and curly, falling freely on his back and shoulders with a few curls falling on both sides of his forehead, and the locks behind his ears are attractively styled into mod-zulfein, stylish curls.

His sartorial style speaks of his fastidious fine taste. A wine coloured long-bodiced angrakha made from fine muslin, which, though usually worn on top of a kurta, he carries off today without one, so that a part of his chest is transparently visible through the fabric. Around his neck he wears a black band with a small gold amulet. A violet sash is twisted and wound around his waist, its ends hanging in the front; a crimson gulbadan pyjama, narrow towards the bottom, flaring up to a comfortable width above the knees, with a broad red belt at the waist. Sometimes he wears a single-width pyjama, but whatever his choice, it is always in silk or some other expensive material. As per his quaint habit, he's carrying a thin hedgehog in his arms. The sleeves of his angrakha are cut at the front, so that he can let them hang loose or fold up, as his heart desires. On his head, he wears a gulshan two-

---

[73]Missi was a powder used for cosmetic purposes. It darkened the gums and whitened the teeth.

panelled cap[74] edged with fine lace. It's a large and roomy cap that covers his head comfortably and shows a part of his forehead and hair up to his parting. In short, he was impeccably attired and cut an impressive figure.

When Maulvi Sehbai and I reached, Hakim saheb was in conversation with Saheb-e-alam Mirza Rahimuddin Haya. 'Saheb-e-alam, I'm tired of your chess diagrams. One or two is fine, but a new request every day? How can one deal with that?'

Saheb-e-alam apologetically explained, 'Ustad, what am I to do? The British Resident Bahadur gives me these chess problems that he gets from England and that he has to solve. Some I'm able to solve on my own and send back to him. Those that I'm unable to understand, I bring to you.'

Hakim saheb looked at us as we entered, nodded in reply to our salaam and motioned to us to be seated. 'Take a seat! Take a seat!'

We sat down and he turned back to Saheb-e-alam. 'Miyaan Haya, the problem you have brought today is not very complex in my opinion. You say the red pieces will be checkmated, I say no, the green will be routed. Spread the chessboard and arrange the pieces; I'll show you how. But first, let me talk to Maulvi Sehbai.'

Smoothly and without any conversational wrinkle, he turned to the other person there. 'Miyaan Sakhanand, you should keep waiting. I have issued the order that this lizard won't move from the front wall until it receives its companion from the east. Its mate will come when it will!'[75]

Sakhanand was a hakim, 'Raqam' was his pen name. He lived in Dharampura and was about forty years old. He was a shagird of Shah Nasir for rekhta, and studied geomancy under Momin Khan. He was good looking and well turned out. He was also

[74]Gulshan is a thin netted fabric used to make caps by stitching together panels side by side.

[75]A reference to a geomancy lesson in progress.
Please also read Momin Khan's brief biographical sketch in *Appendix B*.

courteous and gracious in his manner, gentle, cultured and had a sparkling sense of humour. He looked upon his teacher with respectful devotion, in the manner of a loving son, as evidenced by his humble endorsement of Hakim saheb's instructions and words with 'Very good! Very appropriate!'[76]

After finishing with him, Hakim saheb turned to us. 'Arre bhai Sehbai, you haven't been seen in a while. Tell me, is everything fine? And who is this gentleman with you?' he added, gesturing towards me.

Maulvi Sehbai replied, 'He was my student in college, now he has started a printing press. He wants to hold a mushaira there. We're here to trouble you on that account!'

'Please forgive me! Enough is enough; Dehli's mushairas are no longer fit for respectable folks. There's one gentleman who descends with his retinue of followers,[77] none of whom have the sensibility to understand poetry, applauding meaninglessly, emptily uttering, "Wah! Wah!" and "Subhan-allah!" They disturb my mind and distress my heart. They do not understand that...

Saaeb,[78] *do chiiz mii shikand qadr-e sher raa*
tehsiin-e na-shanaas va sukuut-e sukhan shanaas

---

[76]In a traditional ustad-shagird relationship, the student silently learned and absorbed, even when the teacher wasn't explicitly teaching him. It was an accepted practice that the student would patiently await his turn while the teacher completed other immediate tasks, all the while observing and accruing nuggets of knowledge indirectly. Expressions such as these were a sign of humility and unquestioning devotion to the teacher.

[77]Baig's original footnote: This is a reference to Ustad Zauq and the royal princes from the Qila.

[78]Saaeb lived in the seventeenth century and was popularly known as Saaeb of Tabriz or Saaeb of Esfahan. He was a Persian poet and one of the greatest masters of the ghazal form in Urdu/Persian lyric poetry. He was educated in Esfahan, and in 1626–27 CE, travelled to India. Saaeb was received at Shah Jahan's court and also spent a few years in Kabul and Kashmir before returning to Iran. He died in 1677 CE.

Saaeb, two things torment a poet
Praise from the un-knowing, and silence of the knowing.

'The other gentleman carries Hudhud[79] with him everywhere, and for no reason at all, gets other ustads attacked. He desists from entering the fray himself, using his unworthy faithfuls on his behalf. The other day, that creature read a sher that he had written (without any meaning) and that he claimed to be in the style of Ghalib. I can't tell you how punishing that was for me. From where will they write in Ghalib's hue? Let them and their ustad first gain some understanding of Mirza Nausha's shers. Now, about Meer saheb, that is a different matter. He too says some ludicrous and laughable things, but he does not tear into anyone. On the other hand, because of him, the mushaira becomes entertaining. Bhai, for these reasons, I have stopped going to mushairas.'

I pressed on. 'Ustad Zauq and Mirza Nausha have promised to come to this mushaira. Hazrat Zille Subhani will also be sending his ghazal.'

'Every man is his own master; he may come or send his ghazal. I'm afraid I will neither come nor send any ghazal.'

We were talking thus when a merchant from Benaras arrived laden with two bundles of fabrics. Momin Khan's passion for silks was well known and whenever a cloth merchant came to the city, he was sure to pay a visit to Hakim saheb. Also well-known was the fact that if he took a liking to a fabric, Hakim saheb wouldn't let its price get in the way; he would purchase it at once at the quoted price. The cloth merchant now asked his assistant to put down one of the bundles before Hakim saheb. No sooner had the bundle touched the ground than a lizard fell out of it with a soft thud and scurried to climb the wall in front

[79]Baig's original footnote: More details on Hudhud will come later; a strange character he was!

of us. The first lizard that had been inert on the wall now came to life and immediately went up to greet its new companion. Soon enough the pair took themselves off to one side.[80] All of us watched in fascination!

When the lizards had gone, Hakim saheb joyously exclaimed, 'Miyaan Raqam, did you see that?'

Raqam said, 'Yes indeed! I see now that I made a wrong calculation in one square. Forgive me for insisting I was right!'

Hakim saheb dismissed the apology. 'Don't even think about it. To err is human!'

Turning to us, he asserted, 'Miyaan Sehbai, about the mushaira, my reply is quite firm!'

My heart sank. Khan saheb was proving to be difficult. Then I remembered Nawab Zain ul-Abidin Khan's final word of advice—to employ the weight of his name. I humbly turned to Hakim saheb and entreated, 'Sir, my connection with this mushaira is in name only. Actually, everything is being handled by Nawab Zain ul-Abidin Khan Arif. He is ill, and unfortunately, he feels he doesn't have very long to live. It's his last wish before death claims him, to have an old-style mushaira where Dehli's most accomplished poets are gathered. He might have himself come here, but Hakim Ahsanullah Khan saheb has advised him not to exert himself too much.' This last sentence I added on my own, for good measure.

Finally, I had Momin Khan's attention. He listened to me intently and when I finished, he turned to Maulvi Imam Bakhsh saheb and said in a solemn tone, 'I'm sorry, a real pity! He's such an intelligent and well-meaning man. Such despair at such a young age. Truly, only Allah is forever!' Turning his attention to me, he yielded. 'Achha bhai, please go and tell Arif from my

---

[80]Baig's original footnote: This is a real anecdote; the witness to this died about twenty years ago. I (Farhatullah Baig) heard the anecdote from that gentleman first hand.

side that I will certainly be present at the mushaira.'

I ventured another step when I saw that the magic of invoking Nawab Arif's name had worked. 'Nawab saheb has also made a request—if you could bring along Maulvi Sehbai saheb, Mufti Sadruddin saheb[81] as well as Nawab Mustafa Khan Shefta,[82] it would be most kind of you.'

'Miyaan Sehbai is here, I'll tell him right now. As for Aazurda and Shefta, why don't you go to their homes on your way back and tell them personally? You can say I have sent you. And yes, what's the date that has been decided for it? Where will the mushaira be held and what is the tarah you have assigned for it?'

I told him the date and address of the venue, and then went on to narrate my exchange with Hazrat Jahanpanah regarding the tarah.

He responded, 'Our Badshah Salamat is strange. He comes up with new whimsies! Perhaps such a mushaira would never have been held, where no tarah had been assigned. It's good, in a way. Now there's no ground for differences and disagreements. But here's the thing: unless there's some basis for a contest, where's the enjoyment in writing poetry or in reciting it?'

---

[81]Mufti Sadruddin Aazurda (1789–1868 CE) was Delhi's chief sadr amin (an important judicial position in the Company's administration) and a highly respected scholar and poet as well. He was also sadr-us-sudur and mufti of Delhi, and advised on matters relating to Islamic law. In addition, he was associated with Delhi College and often went beyond his official capacity to support college students, tutoring them free of cost and providing them with food and clothing. Mirza Ghalib was deeply deferential towards Mufti saheb. Aazurda, in turn, greatly influenced Ghalib's poetry and intellectual thought.

Amar Farooqui, *Zafar and the Raj: Anglo-Mughal Delhi c. 1800–1850*, pp. 124, 126.

[82]Mustafa Khan Shefta was a close friend of Mirza Ghalib. In 1847, Mirza Ghalib was imprisoned for three summer months. All through the time, Shefta remained steadfast in his support and friendship, and Ghalib remained grateful to him all his life.

Pavan K. Varma, *Ghalib: The Man, the Times*, 2008.

After he had thus closed this transaction, he busied himself with the more pleasing task of looking at the fabrics the merchant had brought, so I bid him salaam and went on my way.

Close to Chitli Qabar, in front of Haveli Azizabadi, stands the house of Mufti Sadruddin Aazurda. Close to it is Matia Mahal, where Mustafa Khan Shefta saheb lives. Upon reaching Mufti Sadruddin's place, I got to know that Shefta was also with him. I thought I couldn't have had a better chance; I would be able to meet them both together at one place, and happy in my thought, I went in.

The house is built in the style of a kothi[83] and it combines the Indian and British forms. The courtyard is moderately large and contains a small canal. There is a double hall in the front and on its sides, two rooms built in the British style. The outer hall has been turned into a room by putting a door. The halls open on to a terrace on which are placed divans, accoutred in sparkling white covers and gao-takiyas on two sides. When I reached, Mufti Sadruddin Aazurda and Nawab Shefta were seated on the divan seats and immersed in conversation.

Mufti saheb is about fifty-six or fifty-seven years old. A little plump and tawny complexioned, he has small deep-set eyes. With a full beard, he has the look of a straightforward and no-frills man, one who would have nothing to do with outward show. He had on a single-width white pyjama and kurta, and a white turban covered his head.[84]

---

[83]During that era, a kothi or a bungalow was a new architectural style that combined Indian and British stylistic palettes. Aazurda was known to be a mild Anglophile and it is entirely in keeping with his character that his house should be in the kothi style.

[84]Baig's original footnote: In the old days, the wealthy and the nobility were formally dressed at all times, even at home. There were fixed times for going to the zenana, but for the most part, they spent their time in the mardana. There was always someone sitting with them. If they were teachers, then it would be students or

In the city of Dehli, as far as being well turned out was concerned, after top-ranked Hakim Momin Khan came the suave thirty-nine- or forty-year-old Nawab Mustafa Khan Shefta. His swarthy complexion, sharp features and full dark beard came together in an eminently pleasing manner. He was of medium height and heavy build. He was attired in a narrow-bottomed white pyjama, a white kurta and a low-bodiced white angrakha—tasteful, and displaying a pleasing casualness. On his head, he wore a five-panelled panch-goshia,[85] shaped like a dome.

I offered my salutations and then sat on one side of the divan with my feet tucked beneath my thighs. Mufti Aazurda asked me about the purpose of my visit and I conveyed Hakim Momin Khan's message. Mufti saheb heard me out; then, with some astonishment, exclaimed, 'Momin Khan saheb had vowed never to go to a mushaira. Bhai Shefta, what could be the matter? Where on the one hand he had sworn never to attend any mushaira, and now he's dragging others with him?!'

For the second time that day, I spoke about Nawab Zain ul-Abidin Khan Arif and his condition. Mufti saheb listened

---

other intellectuals. If they were poets, then the talk would be about poetry; or, with special friends, conversations on topics of common interest. Wherever one went, there would be a veritable durbar, everyone sitting with folded legs. No needless chatter whatsoever, and no superfluous responses. If someone said something funny, the correct response would be a small smile creasing the face. To burst out laughing loud, or to speak out of turn, or a lot, or to speak in a loud voice were all considered ill-mannered and khilaaf-e-adab (going against the decorum).

[85]The panch-goshia or five-panelled cap was the design creation of Nawab Nasiruddin Haidar, the nawab of Awadh in the 1830s. It ended up becoming quite the rage. In the panch-goshia style, long conical sections were joined and attractive crescent-shaped patterns were sewn on at the rim. These crescents, made of cotton, were stitched on the inside of fine muslin panels. They showed through the panels and produced a simple but eminently elegant effect. This soon became the preferred style of headgear and attained much popularity in Delhi and Lucknow. *Indian Horizons*, Vol. 63, No. 2, April–June 2016.

and said softly, 'So, this is the thing. Now I see! Really, I was taken quite by surprise that Hakim Momin Khan was going to a mushaira.' He added, 'Accha bhai, please tell Arif that Shefta and I will certainly be there.'

When I got out of there, I felt I had successfully completed a huge task, like having bathed in the River Ganga and attained salvation. Feeling elated, I returned and narrated the day's proceedings to Nawab Zain ul-Abidin Khan and he also looked satisfied. When I recounted Momin Khan's initial firm refusal to attend and then his dramatic turnaround, tears sprang to Nawab Arif's eyes. He said, 'Miyaan Karimuddin, do you know, Hakim saheb and I have had a falling out and haven't properly made up?'

I was startled at this revelation. 'Do you really mean that, Nawab saheb? When he heard of your ill-health, he was so deeply affected, I can't tell you. It was as if he had heard the news of his own brother's illness. It was only later that I got to know from Mufti Aazurda that he had taken a vow never to go to a mushaira. He broke his vow only for you!'

'Miyaan! What do you know of the generous affections of these people?' Nawab saheb declared with deep emotion. 'These people are such they cannot bear to see even their worst enemies in any kind of trouble. Anyway, let it go. Now tell me, have you vacated your house?'

I said, 'Yes sir! My house is completely empty now. And if you'd kindly permit, I could also lend you a helping hand.'

Nawab saheb gently brushed aside my offer of help. 'I'd rather you stay away,' he said. 'Whenever two people take on a task together, it's bound to flounder. You leave this arrangement to me, I'll manage it. In fact, I'd go so far as to suggest that you shouldn't venture that side at all. If you were to nitpick while I'm in the middle of the arrangements, it would only end up increasing my work two or three times over.'

Arrangements for the mushaira

ba shair-o-sukhan majlis aaraastand
nishastand-o guftand va barKHaastand

This gathering of poetry and poets is adorned
They assemble, versify, then disperse.

I got so deeply engrossed in translating *Tareekh-e-Abul Fida* that I didn't step out of my house at all for seven or eight days. Zain ul-Abidin Khan saheb was totally absorbed with preparations for the mushaira. Notwithstanding his ill-health and frailty, he would leave his house in the morning and get back late at night by about eight or nine. As a result, I wasn't able to meet him or ask about his well-being. In any case, these eight days passed in the blink of an eye until finally the day of the mushaira dawned, 14 Rajab. At about seven-thirty in the evening, I got ready to go. When I enquired about Nawab Arif, I got to know that after he'd left in the morning, he had not returned.

As I stepped out of the house, I was pleasantly surprised to find that there was quite a buzz in the marketplace. Everyone seemed to be talking about the mushaira. Someone asked, 'Who is this miyaan Karimuddin?' Someone else replied, 'What does it matter who he is, but the arrangements he has made gladden the heart.'

I listened to these exchanges and felt a secret joy. And so, in this state, I reached Hauz Qazi. And what do I see there?

Bamboo screens are hung on both sides of the road with open glass lamps affixed on them at intervals, lighting up the street and turning night into day. Water carriers have nicely sprinkled water on the road to settle down the dust, and their metal bowls are ringing with busy frequency. The main entrance of Begum Mubarak al-nisa's haveli is an illuminated garden, embellished with glass lamps, paper lanterns and sparkling lights. The eyes are blinded by all the dazzle and brightness from the main entrance to the threshold of the house.

When I step inside the house, I am struck dumb. *Ya Allah! Is this my house or have I come to someone else's grand mansion?* I looked all around, wide-eyed, telling myself, 'Wah, miyaan Arif! What wonders you have worked! Where that poor man Karimuddin's humble house, and where this royal magnificence! Indeed, you were right...two thousand rupees would not be too much for this amazing transformation.'

The entire house had been freshly whitewashed with limestone so that the walls and the ceilings gleamed. The courtyard had been filled up and carefully levelled; then large wooden seats had been arranged so as to level the courtyard with the porch. The seats were entirely covered with mats and sparkling white sheets, with exquisite carpets covering the sides and rows of gao-takiyas arranged at the back. It was a palace of light, filled with a profusion of chandeliers, globes, wall lamps, Chinese lanterns, open glass lamps and all manner of radiance. Every single object had been chosen and placed with discerning taste and loving care.

Towards the front and in the centre, a green velvet canopy had been erected on a square frame and was fastened with green silk ropes to ganga-jamni poles in its four corners.[86] Beneath the

---

[86]'Ganga-jamni' is how the author describes the poles—in this context, it stands for golden and silvery. It is a term, however, that has a deeper connotation of syncretism and cultural amalgamation, a sense of harmony that transcends all manner of differences.

canopy was set out a square-shaped green velvet upholstered masnad with matching green velvet gao-takiyas—this was the royal seat of honour. Two silver lanterns with elegant green shades were hung on each of the poles holding up the canopy. Thick jasmine braids hung from the golden dome-shaped tops of the poles, all the way down to the ground, like a bridegroom's sehra. The lower parts of these flower braids had been gathered together and tied to the poles with golden tassels that had shiny metallic beads at their ends, such that there were four jasmine-framed doorways leading into the canopy.[87]

Turning my attention to the walls, I saw that they too were bedecked with garlands of flowers, fastened either to existing pegs or to newly-drilled iron nails. Overhead, a white cloth with an ornate green border had been stretched right from one end to the other, forming an attractive white and green roof. Garlands of white jasmine descended from the centre of this roof, twisted and shaped into an umbrella of flowers.

In one of the small courtyards, there was a provision for water—fresh pitchers along with smaller pewter ewers, all filled with cool water. In another small courtyard, paan were being prepared. In the kitchen, all the paraphernalia for huqqas was meticulously arranged. Properly attired attendants could be seen here and there, standing in respectful anticipation with folded hands. All through the house wafted waves of fragrances, perfumes and incense, now swelling, now fading. Huqqas were lined up along the carpet at regular intervals; all sparkling clean like they had just been bought from the shop. Low three-legged stools stood in between the huqqas with a khaas-daan, betel box, kept on each; in the khaas-daan, betel cones in a wrapping of fine red cloth placed on a fragrant lining of flowers; beside the khaas-daan, a shallow receptacle with the customary snack of cardamom, betel-nut and roasted coriander seeds.

[87]Baig's original footnote: Green was the colour of royalty in Dehli.

Two silver lamp-stands with light-green shades and containing camphor-coated wicks were placed in front of the masnad. These ceremonial lamps were held in silver basins containing kewra, to distil its fragrance. I felt as if I were in a fantasy land, Abul Hasan in *Alf Layla.*[88] Whatever my eyes fell on, they fell in love with it.[89] I was lost in this dreamlike visual feast before my eyes when the stream of arrivals began. The first on the scene was Mirza Karimuddin Rasa. He is about seventy years old and is a salatin.[90] He is only modestly learned, but is convinced that few can match his calibre in poetry. He is a kind-hearted man who is affable and uncomplicated in general.

The proverbial quibble of a boatman about a passenger who is the first to get on the boat and the last to disembark applies to Mirza Rasa in the context of a mushaira. Like the longest-journeying man on the boat, Mirza Rasa is the first to arrive at a mushaira and the last to depart, after every single person has left. It so happened one time that a mushaira was in progress, and all at once, dark and angry rain clouds gathered overhead in the sky. The mushaira was brought to a hurried close and everyone started to leave to be able to get back home before the lowering clouds made good their threat. Mirza saheb, bound by his habit, did not leave his seat. He would, however, from time to time, lean out to catch a glimpse of the heavens and their

[88]*Alf Layla wa-Layla* is the full title in Arabic, and it is known to the English-speaking world as *One Thousand and One Nights.*

[89]Baig's original footnote: Whatever I (Farhatullah Baig) heard from elders who had attended mushairas in the Diwaan-e Aam; I have laid out this mushaira in the very same aesthetic manner.

[90]The salatin were Mughal princes and relatives of the former Mughal emperors. They lived in their own quarters behind a high wall within the Red Fort, an arrangement that allowed them to remain under the watchful eye of the current emperor. By Bahadur Shah's time, these basic quarters had become mean and wretched hovels, and were overcrowded because of the salatin's swelling numbers.

portent. Soon enough it began to pour, and it poured so hard that the entire city sank under sheets of water. After about two hours, the rain let up a bit and he rose to go home. After this much rain, the darkness that fell was so intense, nothing at all was visible, and the house owner solicitously sent an attendant with a lamp to escort Rasa home. Rainwater clogged the streets outside, covering the ankles, and Mirza saheb was now faced with a serious dilemma. How was he to walk through all the hidden puddles and slush in the expensive zardozi shoes he was wearing? Sheepishly, Mirza saheb asked the servant to give him his own shoes. The servant's shoes were raggedy, but Rasa hauled those rags through the puddles while his own gold-embroidered shoes remained safely tucked under his arm. Upon reaching the Qila, he gratefully gave a new pair of shoes to the servant and told him, 'My good man, you have done me a great favour today; I won't forget it all through my life. If you ever need anything, come to me.'

The servant troubled Mirza saheb no end after that fateful day. First, he publicised the incident widely; second, he made it a practice to go to Mirza Rasa every third or fourth day to ask for one or two rupees. Mirza saheb, always the gentleman, never declined and the servant never came back empty-handed.

Nawab Zain ul-Abidin Khan came forward to welcome him and asked why miyaan Haya had not come with him. Mirza Rahimuddin Haya is Mirza Rasa's older son, but for some time now, father and son have had a falling-out. Nawab saheb had only to ask this question, that like a raw wound, Saheb-e-alam Mirza Rasa burst out and words flowed freely, 'Why indeed would he accompany me? Ever since he has come back from Benaras, he's another person. Forget about me, he doesn't think any person merits his attention now. I raised him, fed him, made him a man, gave him an education, trained him in poetry, taught him the art of quail fighting,[91] and I swear on the throne,[92] I gave him all the winning tricks for quail fighting, such that none would know of, whether in the Qila or all of Hindustan,[93] no man nor even the angels. And now, that very "sahebzada" is "saheb", and forget about acknowledging me as his ustad, he even shies away from owning me as his father. Well, why not, it is, after all, the thirteenth century![94] Sending him to Benaras has given me no end of trouble—first, financial loss, and then, the neighbours who take pleasure in my emotional turmoil. Not only has my son gone out of hand, but also there's constant friction, night and day.'

Even as miyaan Rasa carried on in this vein, Nawab Arif led him to his place and asked him to be seated.

He had only just finished with Rasa when a group of princes landed up with Hafiz Abdul Rehman Ehsaan in their midst. Now, is there anyone in Dehli who does not know Hafiz Jeo, ustad to the whole world? There was a time when the entire Qila was his shagird, but the instant Ustad Zauq set foot within the Qila, Hafiz Jeo lost his hold. But then, Jeo understood the ways of the world.

---

[91]Quail-, partridge- and cock-fighting were daily pastimes; it wasn't an unusual sight to see princes from the Qila strut about with their prized quails and partridges perched on their shoulders.

[92]Baig's original footnote: The near-constant intrigues and squabbles that simmered in the palace had seeded royal ambition in the heart of every single prince in the Qila. Every single one of them dreamed of one day wearing the Mughal crown. As a result, the royal family members, whether the heirs or the salatin, all had taken to swearing upon the taj (crown) or the takht (throne).

[93]'Hindustan' refers to the present-day states of Delhi, Haryana, Uttar Pradesh and parts of Bihar and Madhya Pradesh where Hindustani is spoken. 'India' was rarely used in nineteenth-century Urdu sources, but people strongly identified 'Hindustan' as a unit with Delhi as its political nucleus. William Dalrymple, *The Last Mughal: The Fall of a Dynasty, Delhi, 1857*, p. 21n.

[94]The thirteenth century of the Islamic calendar was seen as a prelude to the end of the world that was predicted to come about in the fourteenth century. In everything, therefore, whether small or big, people saw signs of the imminent end of the world.

Long ago in his own youth, he had similarly competed with the eminent Shah Nasir; now in his old age, he did not hesitate to take up the gauntlet. He maintained that he would keep up his fighting spirit until his last breath. He was close to ninety years of age and was bent double like a bow. Even now, however, he was capable of making an impression at a mushaira with his rousing and crisp delivery. His ustadi was a gold coin that had carried weight all over the city for the better part of an era. In the beginning, he had been ustad to Mirza Neeli, then by and by, he ascended to the status of being ustad to Badshah Shah Alam Ghazi.[95] Shah Alam used to address him as 'Hafiz Jeo' and that was how he came to be known in the Qila. He excelled at joining lines and in the art of repartee, leaving his critics speechless. One day in times gone by, Badshah Salamat recited a line:

sub.h bhi bosa to deta mujhe ai maah nahiiN

O moon (the beloved), if only you would also give me a kiss at dawn…

Hafiz Jeo joined it with the following response:[96]

na-munasib hai miyaan vaqt-e-sahargah nahiiN
Not appropriate miyaan, no place of enchantment is the dawn!

---

[95]Shah Alam II, Bahadur Shah's grandfather, became king of a hopelessly depleted Mughal empire in 1760 CE. In 1788 CE, when Zafar was a boy of thirteen, the Rohilla marauder Ghulam Qadir attacked Delhi, blinded Shah Alam II and made Zafar's father, the future emperor Akbar Shah II, dance for his pleasure. In a final insult, he carried away Shah Alam's fabulous library, most of which he sold to the Nawab of Awadh.

William Dalrymple, *The Last Mughal: The Fall of a Dynasty, Delhi, 1857*, pp. 36–37.

[96]This is called 'misra lagaanaa' or joining lines, a 'highly regarded technical exercise'. It is the test of a poet's innate talent and craftsmanship. For example, a young Amir Khusrau was once asked to extemporise a quatrain embedding four completely disconnected things: hair, egg, arrow and melon. Frances W. Pritchett, *Nets of Awareness: Urdu Poetry and its Critics*, p. 85.

Somebody raised an objection to a word he used, but he was quick to quote a couplet by Saaeb to defend his usage, and left the objector speechless. Hafiz Jeo was skinny and had a very dark complexion; Shah Nasir is said to have jested about it thus:

ai KHaal-e-ruKH-e yaar! tujhe THiik banaataa
par chhoD diya hafiz-e-Quran samajh kar

O mole on the face of a friend! I could have made you properly
But let you be for being a hafiz of the Quran.[97]

Nawab saheb took them in hand and ensured that they were given appropriate places. Soon after, Munshi Muhammad Ali Tishna arrived, completely unclothed and drunk, swaying as he entered. He is a young man, and rather strange; sometimes he goes about like this, naked, and other times, he is all dressed up like a gentleman. He is nobody's shagird and still, everyone is his teacher. Sometimes he goes to Hakim Aaga Jaan Aish to obtain corrections for his poetry, and sometimes he approaches Ustad Zauq with his latest ghazal. He is uncommonly sharp and a great number of shers are on the tip of his tongue. Such is his extraordinary gift of memory that he has only to hear a sher and it is committed to memory. It has also happened that he has memorised a certain ghazal upon hearing it and then gone on to reproduce it as his own in another mushaira, leaving the actual owner bewildered.

Nawab saheb went up to him and asked dryly, 'Munshiji, what colour is this?'

He quipped, 'My true colour! When does the mushaira begin?'

---

[97]A person who memorises the Quran is called hafiz and is accorded a lot of respect for his accomplishment. Another interpretation: A mole on the face is black as was Hafiz Jeo. A mole is also regarded as a hafiz of the Quran.
Courtesy Dr Baidar Bakht.

Nawab saheb answered, 'It's going to start soon. But first, do sit down!'

He went and sat in a corner; miyaan Arif brought a shawl and draped it over him. Tishna promptly threw it off. In the end, he continued to sit in his 'true colour', exactly as he had come in.

At this point, the trickle of arriving poets turned into a steady flow. Nawab Arif saw to it that he welcomed every person personally and then seated him appropriately. Hakim Momin Khan made good his promise, and arrived, accompanied by Mufti Sadruddin Aazurda, Nawab Mustafa Khan Shefta, Maulana Sehbai and also Maulvi Mamluk-ul Ali.[98]

Maulvi Mamluk-ul Ali is a leading scholar and teacher in Dehli College—an extraordinary man. His wisdom and magnanimity of spirit have brought such grace to the college, it's unmatched by any teacher in any era. He is a disciplined follower of sharia, and so, does not himself recite shers. Even so, he has an excellent understanding of poetry. If he appreciates a sher, that sher gains sanction to bow its head at the threshold of eternal life. He must be about sixty years old and is originally from Nanauta, but has been living in Dehli for ages. He's deeply involved in teaching, reading and writing, and all his time is spent in these activities. He rarely goes to mushairas, and I think, he came because Maulana Sehbai dragged him here. Some time back, he got into a spot of trouble with the Resident Bahadur because of his rigidity of religious practice. What happened was that the Resident Bahadur came to the Dehli College for an inspection. In a nod to Mamluk-ul Ali's scholarship and position, the Resident Bahadur went up to him and shook hands with him. While the Resident was present, Mamluk-ul Ali discreetly kept his 'shaken' hand away from his body as if he had touched something impure

[98]Mamluk-ul Ali had translated into Urdu many Arabic works on hadith, history and mathematics. He, along with some of his students, helped launch the madrasa movement from Deoband. He died before the 1857 Uprising.

or unclean. After the Resident Bahadur left, however, he washed his hands carefully, several times over. Unfortunately, somebody from the college carried this tale to the Resident, and naturally the latter was incensed. He had meant the handshake to be a mark of respect to Mamluk-ul Ali, and in return, he had been shown this extreme disrespect. In the end, the matter was put to rest only with the greatest difficulty.[99]

Maulvi Mamluk-ul Ali was also my teacher. I went forward and greeted him with 'Aadaab!' He said, 'Miyaan Karimuddin! I didn't know you had this talent; you have beaten the Dehli-wallahs at their own game. Subhan-allah! Subhan-allah! All these excellent arrangements…makes me very happy! May God give you more strength to accomplish even greater things!'

I humbly countered, 'Maulvi saheb! I'm a greenhorn and really not capable at all. All this that you see has been put together by Nawab Zain ul-Abidin Khan.'

He said in amusement, 'Bhai, this is also interesting. He claims that all the arrangements have been made by you, and you say it is his handiwork. This is like a mutual admiration society, with each of you complimenting the other.'[100]

While we were exchanging this banter, I saw Mirza Nausha alighting from his palanquin. Along with him came others like Nayyar, Alai, Salik and Hazeen. Immediately upon arrival, Mirza Ghalib spotted Momin Khan, went towards him, shook hands and exclaimed, 'Bhai Hakim saheb, I got a letter today from Muhammad Nasir Jan Mahzuun from Azimabad. He sends you

---

[99]Baig's original footnote: This incident was mentioned to me (Farhatullah Baig) by Dr Nazeer Ahmad, but without taking any names. At that time, I (Farhatullah Baig) couldn't believe my ears. But now, I have seen such people with my own eyes.

[100]The Farsi phrase he used goes like this: '*Man turaa haaji bagoyam, tu muraa haaji bago.*'

his warmest salaam.[101] I do wonder though why he suddenly went away to Patna. As Khwaja Mir Dard's grandson, his leaving Dehli does not go down well with me.[102] And now he misses his friends; just see what a sorrowful sher he writes:

na to namah hi na paiGaam-e-zubaani aaya
ah Mahzuun! mujhe yaaraan-e-vatan bhuul gaye

Not even a letter nor any message has arrived
O Mahzuun! Friends from my land have forgotten me.'

He continued, 'Arre bhai, has miyaan Ibrahim not yet arrived? The night in all its glory has come. This mushaira, when will it start?'

Hakim Momin Khan was about to reply when a voice was heard from the entrance, 'As-salaam alaikum!'

Maulana Sehbai said, 'Here you go, Mirza saheb! There's Hafiz Veeraan, the herald-elephant for Ustad Zauq. And look, your friend Hudhud is also with him. Let's see who he attacks with his beak today!'

Hudhud's name is Abdul Rahman and he is from the east. He came to Dehli a few years ago and began to teach Hakim Aaga Jaan Aish's children. He lives there itself. It was on Hakim Aaga Jaan saheb's suggestion that he adopted the pen name 'Hudhud'.[103] Hakim Aaga Jaan Aish also helped him cultivate an

---

[101]Mirza Ghalib and Momin Khan had a close relationship, and here, Mirza addresses Momin Khan with the informal 'tum' rather than the formal 'aap' in the phrase '...tum ko bohat bohat salaam bheja hai!'

[102]Khwaja Mir Dard is considered as 'one of the four pillars of the Urdu language' as per Azad in *Aab-e hayat,* along with Mir Taqi Mir, Sauda and Mazhar. He also had Sufi links through his family and was very well respected in Delhi. He stayed on in Delhi even during the widespread destruction wrought by invaders like Ahmad Shah Abdali and others, and died in Delhi in 1785 CE. Mirza Ghalib's unhappiness at Dard's grandson leaving Delhi is to be seen in that context.

[103]Hudhud is a woodpecker or hoopoe. Hakim Aaga Jaan Aish suggested the pen name 'Hudhud' since according to him, 'poets also need to have a pen name that

apt look—a small goatee beard on the chin, a shaved head and a small pointed turban to top it off. And so, he began to look exactly like a hudhud or a woodpecker. It was through Hakim saheb again that Hudhud gained access to the grand Mughal durbar, and what's more, the Emperor conferred on him an array of delightfully airy titles like 'Tair-ul-Arakain', 'Shahpar-ul-mulk', 'Hudhud-ush-Shora' and 'Minqaar-e-Jang Bahadur'.[104]

When Hudhud first began to attend mushairas that were regularly held in Dehli, his light-hearted and entertaining poetry provided amusement in the gatherings. Later on, he took it too far; he began to take rude potshots at the city's ustads and master poets. I've heard that he did it at the behest of Hakim Aaga Jaan, but whatever it was, it made everyone dislike him. And then, rather than him making fun of other poets, Hudhud became the object of everyone's derision. Hakim Aaga Jaan could not openly come to the defence of his protege because he himself did not have the flair to handle the jibes of the Dehli-wallahs. And so, at each such poetic joust, Hudhud would lose steam and quieten down after a little while.

Mirza Nausha and Hakim Momin Khan were especially at the receiving end, and so when Sehbai alluded to miyaan Hudhud as 'your friend', Mirza Nausha smiled and retorted, 'Bhai, why should I entangle with him? Let's see what happens today. For every pharaoh, there's a Moses. I hear our friend Meer saheb has

---

is witty, enjoyable, subtle and sounds good, and need to be crowned with the glory of pomp and circumstance.' The hudhud was the legendary confidant of King Solomon, 'an auspicious-footed messenger' who carried his letter to his beloved, the Queen of Sheba.

Azad, *Aab-e hayat*, Part Eight, *https://dsal.uchicago.edu/books/PK2155.H8413/457481d5.html*

[104]These may be loosely translated as: 'Bird among Pillars', 'Great Winged One of the Land', 'Hudhud of Poets', 'Beak of War Bahadur'.
Ibid.

something to say in praise of Maulvi Hudhud. If this shahbaz-e-sukhan, this 'great' poet can hold his own today, then I will accept that he has done something truly great.'

While we conversed, Ustad Zauq entered, and along with him came the entire Qila. After exchanging 'saheb salamat' with everyone, they all took their seats. The Qila people and their acquaintances who are connected with the Qila have a particular manner of greeting. They stand upright and raise their right hand to their ear as is done before starting the namaaz,[105] then the hand drops back to their side. And that's their special greeting, the saheb salamat. With the others, they exchange the regular greeting.

The Qila people also stand out in their physical appearance, and one can recognise them instantly. In the royal princes as well as the salatin, their lineage is immediately discernible. An extended neck and aquiline nose on an oblong face with high cheekbones, prominent eyes that are moist and gentle, a well-shaped jawline and a broad forehead. They are dark-skinned and their beard remains thin and sparse on the sides of the cheeks, filled out and thicker on the chin. It is remarkable how they all have the same look; unlikely to be found in any other clan. Surprisingly, from the long-faded time of Amir Taimur until the present, their face and form has not changed. Earlier, everyone from the Qila dressed up in the same way too, but now there has emerged another hue.[106] When Sulaiman Shikoh gained influence

---

[105]It is an initial gesture that indicates the individual's resolve for prayer before actually commencing the namaaz.

[106]Baig's original footnote: In this chapter, the dress and attire of Dehli-wallahs are mentioned at various points, and it seems appropriate that these should be described in some detail so that the reader can picture the mushaira in their mind's eye in all its colour and glory.

Leave aside Mirza Nausha; he builds his separate masjid of one-and-a-half bricks, meaning that he makes his own singular style statement. His cap is completely unique in the entire world, being neither in the Turk style nor the Tatari. To make the cap, the skin (of khwasamor or barra) is stitched such that the circumference of the bottom is slightly larger than that of the top. Then four equal sections are cut and the skin sewn halfway down the cap's length. At the centre on top of the cap, a piece of soft velvet or another dark coloured thick fabric is attached and sewn to the ends of the four segments. Inside the cap, a soft lining of another fabric is put in. That, now, is Mirza Nausha's distinctive cap.

Kulah-e-tatari, this style is very much in vogue these days. In the common man's language, it is called the chau-goshia cap. This has various styles and is worn in many different ways. In the style preferred by the elite, the border comes lower and above it are four sections. These sections are curved like Shah Jahan's arches. These are then joined and stitched together so that the four corners emerge like the star-shaped carambola fruit (kamrakh). There have been a few personalised innovations in this. In one, the border is pushed up and the horizontal length of the sections is made to exceed their height. After sewing them together, the excess fabric is cut and fashioned into pleats. This way, there are eight sides instead of four. For embellishment, thin lace is put at the edge of the border on top and the corners are edged with silk lace (qaituun). The Mughal Emperor would wear such a cap in this pattern, only with a border decorated with small discs of gold and silver (salma sitare) and precious stones prominently set. This kind of cap is worn in many different ways. The princes from the Qila wear the cap with the panels upright. Ordinary people press down the sections from the top. The eight-sectioned cap, when pressed down, ends up with its corners splayed outward beyond the border, and takes the shape of a lotus. This kind of cap is always worn at an angle and one corner presses upon the wearer's left eyebrow.

There is another kind of cap that's in fashion—the arqcheen or arkhcheen. Making this is not difficult. The ends of an oblong cloth are joined and sewn to fit the wearer's head, then some delicate gold lace (gota) is put at the bottom of the cap, pleats added to its top along with a small round stiff cloth. Dehli's two-sectioned cap (do-palrhi topi) is differentiated from the Lucknow style in its size. In the Dehli style, the cap is made so big that it covers the head entirely, whereas in the Lucknow style, it perches jauntily on top of the hair.

Besides these, some people also wear the panch-goshia cap. This has five corners and its cut and look are different from that of the chau-goshia. The top edges above the corners are curved; at the bottom, instead of a stiff border there is gota or lace. Before it is worn, it is shaped and fitted on a wooden frame; when the frame-fitted cap is worn, it resembles the dome of Humayun's tomb!

Among the city folk, the big round chandua topi is much in use. Some of these caps are plain, but some are decorated with tambour work (sozni ka kaam) or tape work (fiite ka kaam). This cap is also set on a wooden frame before it is worn.

Among outfits, the angrakha is a great favourite. The bodice of the angrakha

in the Awadh durbar, a few members of the royal family went and settled there.[107] Some others visit Benaras frequently. Whoever

(choli) is cut low and it reaches down to the waist. Everyone is fond of exercise, and so, to show off the contours of the body, the sleeves are tightly fitted, and some of the more fashion-conscious people cut the sleeves from the front to be able to roll them up from the ends. Only a few wear a kurta beneath the angrakha. The Qila princes put on a jaamavaar or velvet khaftaan over the angrakha. For a formal look, the ends of the sleeves are edged with sable or fur; mostly, however, fine lace edges the sleeves. To fasten the ends of the two sides, there is a string and loop in place of buttons, aptly called 'lover-beloved' (ashiq-mashuuq) or 'spectacles' (chashme). It always has short sleeves. In the Qila, it is called a khaftaan, but this front-open, half-sleeved apparel is called sherwani by the city folk.

On top of the angrakha, a square kerchief folded diagonally into the shape of a triangle is draped over the shoulders; in common parlance, this is called 'arkhcheen'. Tying a knotted-up sash or scarf around the waist is also a fashion style, but not seen frequently.

The pyjama is always made of expensive fabric; most often, striped or floral silk fabric (gulbadan), mixed silk and cotton fabric (mashru), thick glossy silk and cotton (atlas), or other varieties of mixed silk and cotton (guurnat) or ghaltah and thicker fabrics. Old-fashioned people still like to wear a single-width or broad-bottomed pyjama. But fitted and narrow-bottom pyjamas have become quite the rage now.

The Salim shahi juuti (delicate shoes with gold or silver embroidery and attributed to Emperor Jahangir and Sheikh Salim Chishti) has begun to be seen, but the Dehli elite seem to prefer the traditional ghetli juuti (a shoe with a flat sole and upturned toe).

Hardly would there be anybody in town who doesn't carry in his hand, a bamboo stick and a square handkerchief made of longcloth. Great effort is invested in choosing a solid and heavy bamboo stick. Mehndi is applied on it and it is hung in the kitchen until its colour changes and darkens to black, and its weight is boosted like it's been dunked in lead.

Everyone you see walks with a swagger. Everyone you see is well built with a slender waist and broad chest, carrying a well-prepared bamboo. Among the elite, there will be only the rare person who is not fond of exercising and wielding the bamboo and banot. From childhood itself these forms of sport and exercise are taught. Competitions are regularly held, the cheering and wah-wahs provide encouragement to children and young people, and the soldier's occupation becomes a stamp of nobility.

[107]Mirza Sulaiman Shikoh was the brother of Akbar Shah II; he left Delhi and

goes for a visit brings back some new sartorial style and cut, so that his costume becomes aadhaa tiitar aadhaa bater, half partridge and half quail. In the end, he is dressed in a style that's not fully Lucknawi and is different from that of a Dehli-wallah. Now look closely at the persons seated here. The princes who have visited Lucknow wear the Lucknawi do-palrhi topi, the two-sectioned cap on their heads, a high-bodiced angrakha on top of a fine wine-coloured muslin kurta and a narrow fitted pyjama. On the other hand, those that have never set foot outside the Qila wear the same old style of dress: a chau-goshia cap on their head, a low-bodiced angrakha with a velvet or jaamavaar khaftaan on top and a broad-bottomed pyjama made from gulbadan or ghaltah. The Lucknow-travelled princes have also bid farewell to the beard. Their face-cut and look betray their Dehli Mughal lineage, but their style and presentation have the unmistakable stamp of Lucknow.

Meanwhile, the venerable Ustad Zauq went around and greeted everyone, then finally went and sat on the right side of the canopy. In a mushaira, seating the poets in a certain order is also an art. Nawab Zain ul-Abidin Khan deserves praise that he seated each poet as he saw fit, and so smoothly that nobody had any reservations or qualms of any kind whatsoever. If a poet went and sat in a place where Nawab saheb thought the poet shouldn't be seated, rather than asking him outright to get up, Nawab saheb would himself go and sit at the poet's 'proper' seat. After some time, he would call out to the poet in question, 'Arre bhai, my friend, just come here, I want to say something…' The poet would walk over and sit by his side while Nawab saheb would continue talking to him for a bit longer. By then some other person would come in who would be apt for the vacated seat, and Nawab saheb would greet the new entrant, 'Please take

made his home in Lucknow. He lived out his days in comfort and grandeur there, in the benevolent shadow of the Awadh rulers.

your seat, that seat is vacant!' Now that the earlier seat was occupied, he would find an excuse to get up and move on to some other thing. This way, both seats were filled and everyone was dealt with delicately and with the greatest courtesy.

Seating the princes is a trickier proposition, what with their quicksilver temperaments. '*What! You think we should sit here?!*' Then no matter how much you try to make up, they will not come around. Ustad Zauq was well aware of these difficulties and he took it upon himself to manage the seating of the people accompanying him—with gracious understatement, so that nobody felt that he was organising things his own way. To someone he said, 'Saheb-e-alam, please come here.' To someone else, he pointed towards a seat, 'Come bhai, sit there!' In the end and soon enough, the entire mehfil was comfortably settled.

The way the poets had been seated was: to the right of the Mir-e-mushaira were arrayed the people from the Qila, and to the left sat the poets and ustads from the city along with their pupils. One thing I noticed and that I found strange was that all the Qila princes had quails pressed under their arms. I suppose it's because the malaise of quail- and cock-fighting is widespread in the Qila, and every other day, there are contests among quails, partridges, and cocks.

One of the princes has taken his passion to another level. With the aid of bamboo sheets, he has made a little hut on a large wheelbarrow and thrown soil on it. In the soil on the roof of the hut, he has sown barley seeds. God save me if I'm lying, lakhs of small birds have made their home in the wheelbarrow-hut. The prince takes the wheelbarrow with him wherever he goes and lets the birds fly around. The birds are well-trained and do not stray too far. He waves a little flag and off they fly, he calls out to them and they promptly fly back and perch on the roof.

A few minutes after Ustad Zauq came, Mirza Fakhru also arrived in a hawadar, an open palanquin. Nawab Mirza Khan

Daagh was accompanying him.[108] Nawab Mirza Khan Daagh is about sixteen or seventeen years old. His complexion is rather dark, but his face has an endearing softness—large hooded eyes, long straight nose and broad forehead. He wore a black velvet chau-goshia cap edged with fine lace on his head, a silk angrakha and green silk pyjama, and finally, a silk handkerchief in his hand. He is young, but his shers are such that, Subhan-allah, already his ghazals are being sung all over the city!

Mirza Fakhru's palanquin was lined up close to the entrance, then lowered to the level of the porch, and miyaan Daagh stepped out and stood to one side. Then Mirza Fath-ul-mulk alighted. Everyone stood up with the proper ceremonial courtesy. Following the palanquin were four chobdaars formally attired in green turbans with a window-like opening in the front, green-coloured long coats made of a thick cloth teamed with red sashes around their waists. Two chobdaars held ganga-jamni staffs and the other two held fans made of peacock feathers. When Mirza Fakhru stepped out, the staff-bearing chobdaars quickened their pace and positioned themselves some distance in front of him, while the peacock fan-bearers fell behind him without so much as missing a step. The royal procession now moved slowly and gracefully towards the shamiana, the canopy. Mirza Fakhru paused before the shamiana, then turned around and acknowledged the courtesies and greetings of all the guests. Looking around at the gathering, he said, 'Do I have your leave?'

Everyone answered in one voice. 'Bismillah! Bismillah!'

He entered the shamiana, offered his salaam to everyone and

---

[108]Nawab Mirza Khan Daagh was in Mirza Fakhru's care and he lived in the Qila. After the hanging of Daagh's father, Nawab Shamsuddin Khan, the Nawab of Loharu, his mother Wazir Khanum (aka Chhoti Begum) married Mirza Fakhru. Daagh was deeply influenced by Wazir Khanum, a beautiful and accomplished woman, and a poet herself. Her amazing story has been narrated, most lovingly so, by the outstanding and peerless Shamsur Rahman Faruqi in *The Mirror of Beauty*.

took his seat at the centre, on the masnad. The others remained standing, waiting for his consent to return to their places. Mirza Fakhru looked around and requested, 'Tashreef rakhiye! Please take your seats!'

Everyone offered salaam and resumed their seats, familiar with the etiquette. Ustad Zauq motioned to Daagh to come and sit on a seat near him; Daagh immediately complied.

In keeping with the royal protocol, the fan-bearers stood behind the shamiana while the staff-bearers took their position in front of the shamiana, behind the front row. Saheb-e-alam Mirza Fakhru was now flanked by the two sets of attendants, signalling his status as the guest of honour on this most special of occasions for Dehli. After these formalities had been completed, Nawab Zain ul-Abidin Khan Arif came forward towards the shamiana to offer his salutations to Mirza Fakhru, and sat down on folded legs beside him. They conferred in whispers and soon after, Nawab Arif rose and went to his seat a little distance away.

Nawab Fath-ul-mulk Mirza Fakhru then raised both his hands for the Fatiha, and along with him, everyone in the gathering raised their hands in prayerful supplication.[109] After the Fatiha Khair, Saheb-e-alam Mirza Fakhru spoke, 'O mellifluent voices of the garden of Dehli! What is my standing before you, most learned master poets, and how can I even entertain the thought of being the Mir-e-mushaira in your presence? I am here in your service only in obedience to Hazrat Pir-o-murshid's command; else I have no weight to be Mir-e-majlis of this large and luminous mushaira. Dear friends, you are already aware of one special feature of this mushaira, and that is, no tarah has been assigned for it. The other unique feature you will find is that instead of one ceremonial lamp, two lamps will circulate. Just like the taking

[109]Baig's original footnote: Mirza Fath-ul-mulk Bahadur was a strictly observant person and never began any task without chanting the Fatiha Khair the opening verse in the Quran. Everyone in the Qila used to refer to him as 'mullah'.

away of the tarah closed the door on competitive one-upmanship, the circulation of two lamps will alleviate the anxiety in all hearts and minds as to whose turn comes first and who's next. Then there is the matter of who begins and ends the mushaira—that decision, a difficult decision, often paints a wrinkle in friendly ties. In this mushaira, I have brought together the ibtada and the inteha, the start of the mushaira and the zenith of its closure. The outstanding kalaam of Hazrat Zille Subhani will herald the beginning of the mushaira as per custom; thereafter, I will proffer my own ghazal, and in this way, I will erase the difference between the beginning and the end.'[110]

At this, Mirza Fakhru waved his hand and summoned the chobdaars standing in front. Immediately, they picked up the two ceremonial lamps and brought them to him. With a softly-uttered 'Bismillah,' he lighted the lamps after removing their shades and then gently put the shades back. The chobdaars now picked up the illuminated lamps, replaced them in the silver basins and once again returned to their stiff upright positions. They glanced towards Mirza Fakhru who, with an imperceptible nod of the head, gave a sign, upon which the chobdaars announced in ringing tones: 'Hazraat! The mushaira now begins!'

Immediately there fell a pin drop silence in the gathering. The Qila people put their quails into bags and placed them behind the gao-takiyas. The attendants were quick on their feet, taking away the huqqas and putting in their place spittoons, khaas-daan and the plates with cardamom, betel nut and roasted coriander seeds. Afterwards, they stood attentively in their places in the

---

[110]In a mushaira, great value was placed on protocol and decorum. The poets' seating, the order in which they would recite, which senior poet would be given the pride and honour of closing the mushaira with his recitation, how would the poets respond to one another's offerings (response and participation were an integral part), and how would the ustads' sometimes-unruly pupils behave, these were all delicate matters that required close attention and careful calculation.

Frances W. Pritchett, *Nets of Awareness: Urdu Poetry and its Critics*, pp. 70–71.

courtyards, ready for the eventful night to unfold.

Just then a special envoy from the Qila brought Badshah Salamat's ghazal; along with him came several royal heralds. He went up to the ceremonial lamp, offered his salutations and then sought permission to recite the ghazal. Mirza Fakhru gave his assent with a nod of his head. The envoy sat down there itself and the heralds proclaimed in a clear resonant voice: 'Haaziriin! Hazrat Zille Subhani, Saheb-e Qiran-i Sani, Malik-ul-Sultanat's miraculously sublime kalaam is now being read. Please lend your ears with the utmost respect and from the depths of your heart.'

The mushaira unfolds

huzuur-e-shah meiN ahl-e-sukhan ki aazmaish hai
chaman meiN KHush navayaaN-e-chaman ki aazmaish hai[111]

In the royal presence, eloquent men will be put to the test
In the garden, melodious voices of the garden will be put to the test.

Upon the announcement of the royal herald, everyone sat on folded knees, their heads bowed in deferential anticipation of Badshah Salamat's ghazal. The envoy took out the ghazal from his bag, kissed it, touched it to his eyes and then began to recite it in a ringing voice. The theme of the ghazal, its development from one couplet to the next, the expert embroidery of words within the theme, all displayed a magisterial hold on the tongue. Most of all, the melodious recitation in the notes of raag Sorath[112] set the mood for the evening. It seemed as if a shimmering aura, a column of light was woven from earth to heaven, enveloping the whole mehfil. As the ghazal progressed,

---

[111]This verse was written by Mirza Ghalib in 1852. Courtesy Dr Baidar Bakht.

[112]This is an Indian classical raag that appears in the Sikh religious tradition and is part of the Guru Granth Sahib. Guru Nanak and many Sikh gurus composed hymns and songs in this raag. It is a raag that can, by its arrangement of notes and compositions, create a compelling atmosphere.

everyone got deeply absorbed, so much so that nobody even thought about giving praise. The ustads imperceptibly swayed on receiving each couplet and occasionally, a Subhan-allah was heard in a muted whisper. Other than that, there was utter stillness, a glowing net of spiritual wonder mesmerising everyone, and at the maqta, the last couplet, the slow-growing spell was complete. The listeners found themselves in a state of total rapture. The maqta was recited again, and yet again, upon repeated requests from one or the other, to better appreciate the honey sweetness of the words and the layered thought-provoking motif. Come, you also read and savour its sweetness.[113]

nahiiN ishq meiN iska to ranj hameN ke qaraar-o-shakeb zara na raha
Gam-e-ishq to apna rafiiq raha koi aur balaa se raha na raha

na thi haal ki jab hameN apne KHabar, rahe dekhte auroN ke aib-o-hunar
paDi apni buraiyoN par jo nazar, to nigaah meiN koi bura na raha

hameN saaGar-e-baada ke dene meiN ab kare der jo saqi, to hai Gazab
ke yeh ahd-e-nashat, yeh daur-e-tarab na rahega jahaaN meiN sadaa, na raha

lage yuN to hazaaroN hi tiir-e-sitam ke taDapte rahe paDe KHaak pe hum
vale naaz-o-karishma ki teG-e-do-dam lagi aisi ke tasmaa laga na raha

[113]Karimuddin, in his role as a narrator, communicates directly with the reader, and without another thought, the reader becomes part of the magical mushaira unfolding here.

Zafar! aadmi usko na janiyega, ho voh kaisa hi saheb-e-fahm-o-zakaa
jise aish meiN yaad-e-Khuda na rahi, jise taish meiN KHauf-e-Khuda na raha

I sorrow not that in love I did not find solace at all nor any relief
Love's anguish was ever a companion whether or not anyone else was

Mindless of my own I counted the vices and virtues of others
When my eyes fell on my failings then nobody seemed bad

What injustice, the saqi holds back from giving me a cup of wine
This age of excitement, this time of joy are passing shadows in time

I braved a thousand arrows of tyranny that left me flailing in the dust
But the double-edged sword of coyness and pride severed my heart outright

Zafar! Do not deem him a worthy man, no matter how learned and sage
Who fails to hail God in ease and pleasure, and fears Him not in passion and rage.[114]

After having recited the ghazal, the envoy handed the page to Mirza Fakhru—a gold-sprinkled page that had the ghazal written by the hand of Zille Subhani himself. Mirza Fakhru took the

[114]The Badshah's ghazal has a Sufi theme, suffused as it is with spiritual wisdom, while tinged with a breath of melancholy. It has layers of meanings and that gives it a timeless appeal.

pakiizah, the flawless and pure sheet of paper, with the utmost reverence[115] and cast his eyes over the gathering.

Mamluk-ul Ali spoke, with his hand on his heart, 'Saheb-e-alam! How can I even begin to praise Zille Subhani's ghazal in a suitable way? We are indeed honoured that Hazrat Pir-o-murshid is partaking in this mushaira by sending his ghazal and bestowing his noble grace upon us all. I would be grateful if my humble shukriya is conveyed to Hazrat Jahanpanah.'

Mirza Fakhru acknowledged it and looked towards the envoy, who responded, 'Qibla-e-alam, I will communicate it immediately upon arriving at the palace.' Thereafter, he saluted and made to leave, but Mirza Fakhru stopped him as an afterthought. 'Before you go, please also recite the ghazal of Saheb-e-alam Wali Ahad Bahadur.[116] He handed me his ghazal as I was leaving and requested me to have it read by someone with a melodic voice. Who better than you to read it?'

He reached into his pocket to take out a sheet of paper and gave it to the envoy. The latter saluted, and sitting down close by, recited this ghazal.

dil se lutf-o-meherbani aur hai
meherbani ki nishaani aur hai

qissa-e Farhad-o-Majnu aur hai
ishq ki mere kahaani aur hai

---

[115]For his Hindu and Muslim subjects, the mystique and appeal of the Mughal Emperor was as much religious as political. His coronation portrait described him as: 'His Divine Highness, Caliph of the Age, Padshah as Glorious Jamshed, He who is surrounded by Hosts of Angels, Shadow of God, Refuge of Islam, Protector of the Mohammedan Religion, Offspring of the House of Timur, Greatest Emperor, Mightiest King of Kings, Emperor son of Emperor, Sultan son of Sultan'. William Dalrymple, *The Last Mughal: The Fall of a Dynasty, Delhi, 1857*, p. 21.

[116]The reference is to Mirza Fakhru's older brother, Crown Prince Mirza Muhammad Dara Bakht, aka Mirza Shabbo, who died in 1849.

rokne se kab mire rukte haiN ashk
balki hoti KHuuN fiishaani aur hai

hum se ai Dara, voh kab hote haiN saaf
unke dil meiN bad-gumaani aur hai

It's different for the heart to feel the joy of kindness
To display kindness is something else

The tale of Farhad and Majnu is different[117]
The story of my own love is something else

When have my tears abated upon my stopping them
The soul bleeds over and that's something else

When does she open up with me, O Dara![118]
The mistrust in her heart is something else.

It was evident that the ghazal was lightweight, but it was Wali Ahad Bahadur's ghazal and nobody had the heart not to praise it. Of course, Ghalib and Momin remained steadfastly silent. A few of the Qila princes may have felt bad about that, but they also knew that Mirza Ghalib and Momin Khan gave praise only when the poet and his kalaam were truly deserving of it. Empty compliments were not in keeping with their station, and indeed, they never did give accolades that were not fully merited. True, this was Wali Ahad's ghazal; but even if it had been the ghazal of Badshah Salamat himself, and a weak one, their heads would have remained stubbornly still, signalling their real feelings about it. The envoy soon departed, having recited the ghazals of the absent Qila participants, and now it was the

[117]The myths of the famously star-crossed lovers Shirin-Farhad and Laila-Majnu were written by the twelfth-century Persian poet Nizami Ganjavi, master of the masnavi style. These are long narrative poems in which the lovers are continually thwarted and death is seen as a deliverance from the disillusionment of this world.

[118]'Dara' was the pen name of Mirza Shabbo.

turn of those present at the mehfil to recite their ghazals.

On Mirza Fakhru's cue, the chobdaar brought the lamps and placed them before the shamiana. Mirza Fakhru took out his ghazal, scanned the audience, then slightly tilted his head and with some hesitation said, 'What is my locus standi that I can bring myself to recite before you, all poets and ustads, accomplished masters of your craft. Well, whatever I have written, good or bad, I present before you with an aim to receive your comments and criticisms.

Gam voh kya hai jo jaaN guzaa na hua
dard voh kya jo laa-davaa na hua

haal khul jaayeN Gair ke saare
par karuuN kya ke tu mera na hua

dard kya jis meiN kuchh na ho tasiir
baat kya jis meiN kuchh mazaa na hua

voh to miltaa par ai dil-e-kamzarf
tujh ko milne ka hauslaa na hua

shikva-e-yaar aur zabaan-e-raqiib
khel THehra koi gilaa na hua

tum raho aur majme' aGyaar
mera kya hai hua hua na hua

phir tumhare sitam uTHane ko
Ramz achha hua buraa na hua

What is that sorrow if it doesn't hollow out the soul
What ache is that if it isn't beyond cure

All of a stranger's secrets spill out before me
But what should I do if you still elude me

What good is pain if it doesn't remake a man from within
What use is something that brings no relish

She would have met you, but you, witless man
Did not have the courage to meet her

The beloved's complaints or a rival's words
Are merely in play, no complaints at all

Stay, remain in the crowd of your admirers
What difference is it if I remain or depart

To be able to again put up with your tyrannies
Ramz only got better; it wasn't so bad.'

Mirza Fakhru did not have a loud voice, but his rendition of the ghazal was drawn from the heart—it touched the audience's heart at once. The mehfil was echoing with cries of wah-wahs and Subhan-allah as he drew to the end. The third sher elicited a passionate round of praise from Mirza Ghalib, and the fifth sher from Hakim Momin Khan; they spontaneously left their seats as they showered unreserved applause. Even as Mirza Fakhru proceeded with the reading, they repeated those couplets, again and yet again, to relish their poetic artistry.

Finally, the ghazal came to an end and Mirza Nausha lauded him with heart-warming words. 'Subhan-allah! Saheb-e-alam, Subhan-allah! What a ghazal! The way you read the shers, it was a treat for the senses.'

Ustad Zauq smiled as if to say, 'Chalo, I'm being given praise, even if indirectly!'[119]

Mirza Fakhru rose and bowed before the mehfil. 'This is your generous affection as elders that you encourage me thus.' In a self-effacing manner, he added the Persian adage, 'I am what I know I am!'

---

[119]Like a true teacher, Ustad Zauq took pride in the appreciation his pupil got from the master poets, with whom he had a contentious relationship that played out in different ways from time to time.

The entire mehfil was now abuzz with a great many exclamations of appreciation, and Mirza Fakhru acknowledged them all with gracious bows and salaams. After a few minutes, order was restored in the gathering. Mirza Fakhru gestured to the chobdaar and he removed one lamp from its place before the canopy and placed it before miyaan Yal in the front row. His real name was Abdul Qadir, but even children on the street addressed him as miyaan Yal.[120] He was a wrestler, and so vain about his physical prowess that he didn't consider any other wrestler in the city to be his match.[121] There were several wrestling arenas in Dehli, and

---

[120]'Yal' literally means a big, strong and brave man.

[121]Baig's original footnote: Ultimately, it was his arrogance that brought him down. His daily challenges to the wrestlers in the wrestling arenas, for no reason other than to flaunt his vanity, were becoming insufferable. The ustad of the Sheikhowalon wrestling arena, Haji Ali Jaan, trained a young wrestler with the specific objective of taking on miyaan Yal. This young man wasn't very muscular or well-built, but his tackling technique was good and he was nimble and quick on his feet.

One day when Yal arrived at the arena and as per his habit threw an open challenge, the youth got to his feet and went up to Yal to shake his hand. Yal was amused at this and held back from taking his hand. Ustad Haji Ali chided him, 'Why this hesitation to shake his hand? Either you shake hands with him today or never again come here to challenge a wrestler.' Yal asked him why he was pitting this weakling against him knowing full well he'd get pummelled at Yal's hands. Ustad Haji Ali Jaan quipped, 'Miyaan, as you sow, so shall you reap! On the fateful day, you can pound him to pulp. What is the most that will happen? You will break his hands and legs, and he will learn his lesson for the future.'

Ultimately, the two shook hands and a date was fixed for the bout. It was scheduled a couple of days after this mushaira, at the royal wrestling ground, near the idgah. The ground had seating for ten to fifteen thousand persons, but on the day of the big fight, the ground was jam-packed and wherever you turned, you could see only heads, and more heads. Thanks to Yal's great unpopularity, the entire Dehli city had turned up to watch the bout, and all were on the side of Yal's young challenger.

After a few other minor bouts, exactly at four o'clock, Yal and the young man entered and the fight began. Sprinkling mud on their chests, muttering a prayer, they stood face to face. They were as oppositely built as the earth and sky, and it seemed like a contest between an elephant and an ant. A pin drop silence descended

wherever he went, he would throw an open challenge that no wrestler could find the courage to accept. In fact, it was because of his great passion for wrestling that he had chosen this pen name, 'Yal'. His choice of theme was similarly aggressive, and his style of recitation, as if he were reciting a war poem. He did not concern himself with appreciation or words of praise from the gathering. His job was over with the reading of his ghazal. He had written this ghazal:

keh do raqiib se ke voh baaz aaye jang se
hargiz nahiiN haiN yaar bhi kam us dabang se

lab ka baDHa diya mazaa KHitta-e-sabz ne
saqi ne pusht dii mai-e-saafi ko bang se

dil ab ke be-tarah se phaNsaa zulf-e-yaar meiN
nikle yeh kyuN ke dekhiye qaid-e-farang se

aa jaaiyo na pech meiN zaalim ke dekhna
yaari to tum ne kii hai Yal, us shoKH-o-shang se

Tell the opponent to give up the fight
The lover is no less daring than him

This time the heart is hopelessly caught in tangled tresses
How will I free myself from the firangi's clutches

---

on the crowd. The encounter commenced. All of miyaan Yal's power-packed moves were countered dexterously by the youth with immense agility of his thin body. At one point, Yal overpowered the boy completely and pinned him to the ground. It seemed like the end. But by employing small and strategic moves, the boy managed to disentangle himself, and at some point, like lightning, he tripped miyaan Yal, threw him to the ground and sat riding his chest, proclaiming a decisive victory.

Jubilant shouts rent the air. Overjoyed people ran into the ground and picked up the youth in their arms in awe-struck, congratulatory joy. Nobody cared to see where Yal was lying and what his condition was. Miyaan Yal silently sneaked out with his face covered and was never seen again. It is believed he left Dehli for good, and nobody knew what became of him or where and how he died.

Don't be deceived by her cunning manoeuvres
O Yal, you have loved someone playful and clever.

After his ghazal was done, the chobdaar picked up the second lamp and placed it before Mirza Ali Baig. He is a fair and good-looking young man, fond of exercising. He is the only rekhti-go[122] in Dehli and writes under the pen name 'Nazneen'. Meanwhile, Nawab Zain ul-Abidin Khan called out for an odhni.[123] An attendant immediately produced a lovely star-encrusted crimson scarf. Nazneen draped it with elaborate delicacy, one end thrust into his side and the other spread in the front, making a very good impression of a pretty woman. He performed his ghazal with such coyness that the entire gathering was chuckling with sumptuous amusement. His dancing was more beautiful than a dancing girl's, and his reading of the second couplet was as if he would go to any extent to make baaji (sister) jealous.[124] The Qila people were delighted with the ghazal, but the ustads of rekhta maintained a stony silence. This was how it went:

hui ushshaq meiN mashhuur Yusuf-sa javaaN taakaa
bua! hum auratoN meiN tha baDaa diidah ZuleKHa ka

---

[122]Rekhti is the feminine of rekhta, and usually refers to poetry written by male poets in the female voice and using the female idiom in Lucknow in the late eighteenth and nineteenth centuries. Saadat Yaar Khan Rangin, Inshallah Khan Insha and Mohsin Khan Mohsin popularised rekhti. Ruth Vanita's *Gender, Sex & the City: Urdu Rekhti Poetry in India, 1780–1870* (London: Palgrave Macmillan, 2012) is the first book-length study in English on rekhti.

[123]Odhni or dupatta is a long scarf made from two metres or more of silk or other transparent and fine fabric, and embellished with delicate embroidery or various kinds of elaborate work. It is worn by women in various styles, either draped across the shoulders and the front, or in the manner of the end of a sari.

[124]A rekhti-go would recite, or rather, perform his rekhti by mimicking a woman, not just in dress and mannerisms, but also in the subject of the piece, vocabulary and style.

mujhe kehti hai baaji tuune taakaa chhoTe devar ko
nahiiN darne ki maiN bhi, haaN nahiiN taakaa to ab taakaa

agar Nazneen tu dubli-patli kaamni-si hai
chhareraa sa badan naam-e-Khuda hai tere dauha ka

Yusuf was famed for his beauty among admirers
Among us women Zuleikha was more sought after

My sister tells me I gazed at her brother-in-law
I'm not afraid, if I haven't until now, I will look now

If Nazneen you are petite and pretty
God's name has the grace of a shade-giving tree.

Now the two lamps were circulating in a set fashion—one poet on the right side would read his ghazal, followed by a person on the left.

I have included a figure to give the reader an idea of the arrangement of the poets, the order in which their turn to recite would come and, in general, the organisation of the mushaira.[125]

[125]Once again, Karimuddin is drawing the reader into his world with his direct tone and a visual depiction of the seating of poets.

Bismil (23)	Bedil (25)	Shauq (27)	Tasalli (29)	Naalaan (31)	Maaher (33)	Fusoon (35)	Ashki (37)	Hashmat (39)	Ijad (41)
Jafri (21)									Rasa (43)
Tanveer (19)									Rifat (45)
Yakta (17)									Qana'at (47)
Josh (15)									Haya (49)
Tajalli (13)									Zahir (51)
Kamil (11)									Sabir (53)
Qalq (9)									Daagh (55)
Tasveer (7)									Ehsaan (57)
Auj (5)									Zauq (59)
Nazneen (3)									**Mirza Fakhru Ramz** (1)
Yal (2)									Ghalib (58)
Aashiq (4)									Momin (56)
Tamkeen (6)									Aazurda (54)
Taabish (8)									Shefta (52)
Auj (10)									Sehbai (50)
Ta'ashshuq (12)									Aish (48)
Raqam (14)									Arif (46)
Aziz (16)									Rakhshan (44)
Shohrat (18)									
Hazeen (20)									Alai (42)
Tishna (22)	Taskeen (24)	Taib (26)	Azad (28)	Shor (30)	Meer Saheb (32)	Barq (34)	Huzoor (36)	Betaab (38)	Salik (40)

Seating arrangement for the poets in Dehli's last mushaira. The numbers in parentheses show the order in which the poets recited their ghazals. Mirza Fakhru, on the right side, is first to recite, and Ustad Zauq, seated next to him, recites in the end. Before Mirza Fakhru, the ghazals of the Badshah and Wali Ahad are recited by an envoy, because as per protocol, they cannot be present at this mushaira.

Courtesy: Dr Baidar Bakht

After Nazneen, the lamp moved to the right to miyaan Ashiq. He is a working man, quite uneducated, and is nobody's shagird or ustad. He does, however, write good poetry, and in this mushaira, one couplet of his earned him a lot of appreciation. The remaining couplets in his ghazal were merely a foil to this particular couplet that got spectacular success:

faqat tu hi na mera ai but-e-KHuuN KHaar dushman hai
tire kuuche meiN apna har dar-o-divaar dushman hai

Cruel beloved! You are not my only enemy
Every wall and doorway in your lane is my enemy.

After he had finished, the left-hand lamp came to Abdullah Khan Auj. An experienced and expert poet, about forty to forty-five years of age, he combs the poetic universe for rare mazmuuns[126] and ever-elusive meanings. His deep explorations end in success when he is able to unveil a new motif or thought. Often, the full explication of it requires a complete ode, one couplet being woefully insufficient to carry the full weight of the subject. But he attempts to cram the whole interpretation into a single sher and ends up conveying something quite different. How will the listeners enjoy his poetry then, and give any praise? It often turns out, therefore, that he recites the ghazal, enjoys its light and shades of meanings, and ultimately, ends up praising himself too. His recitation is particularly enthusiastic and when he's in flow, he forgets himself and goes ahead of his seat by a

[126]A mazmuun may be understood as a thematic thread from some part of the poetic universe—an endless ocean that is constantly being plumbed by poets for new pearls, or old pearls shining with new meanings. There were some poets, however, like miyaan Auj, who kept up an obsessive quest for novelty, for novelty's sake alone. Such poets were reproached by other poets for their 'Khayaal-bandi' or 'nazuk-khayaali', and their torturous overworking of a theme was met with much criticism. For more, see Frances W. Pritchett, *Nets of Awareness: Urdu Poetry and its Critics*, pp. 94–95.

few yards. He has only a few pupils, but the ustads regard him no less than a full ustad. Who has the nerve, after all, to deny his mastery and invite his ire? Barely does he finish reading his ghazal than a laudatory wah-wah bursts out from Ustad Zauq or Mirza Ghalib. This is a necessary reaction, else miyaan Auj gets annoyed and that produces a difficult situation for one and all. This was the ghazal he read:

dam ka jo damdamaa yeh baandhe khayaal apna
be-pul-e Siraat utreN yeh hai kamaal apna

tiflii hi se hai mujh ko vahshat-saraa se nafrat
sum meiN gaDHa hua hai aaho ke naal apna

kasbe-shahaadat apna hai yaad kisko qaatil
saNche meiN teG ke sar lete hain Dhaal apna

chechak ke aablon ki maiN baag moDta huN
(rakh ke) devi ke aastaaN par siimiiN hilaal apna

The power of my poetic-thought can propel me with ease
Over the razor-edge of Pul-e-Siraat as if it didn't exist

From my childhood I hated the dreary desolation of desert lands
Sadly my navel cord tethers me to the musk deer's wanderlust

Where all I was martyred how can I recall, my killer!
My head has been moulded in the cast of the sword

I make the smallpox blisters subside and dry
Laying my silver head on the threshold of the goddess.[127]

---

[127]This ghazal is a busy place. There's the Pul-e-Siraat or the bridge between hell and paradise, described in the Quran as being thinner than a strand of hair, sharper than a sword and hotter than hellfire. There's also the musk deer, that in myth, wanders in the desert endlessly, crazed by the perfume in its navel. There's the reference to smallpox and the ritual of appeasing the goddess Sheetla Mata for its

At the last couplet, Mirza Ghalib jumped up and exclaimed, 'Wah miyaan Auj! The second line of the last couplet is out of this world! Vallah! How well you have wedged the words! All these that call you "ustad" are really kafirs. I say, miyaan, you are the God of poetry!'[128]

All the other masters too, voiced much praise, albeit superficial, but here we have miyaan Auj lapping it all up and swelling with pride.

When silence regained ground, the right-side lamp slid to the side of Muhammad Yusuf Tamkeen. He is about fifteen or sixteen years old and studies at the Dehli madrasa. He has a delightfully jocular manner and is polite and well-spoken. With his nicely formed delicate features and wheatish complexion, he promises to grow up into a handsome young man. This was his ghazal:

dozaKH bhi jisse mangtaa har dam panaah tha
kis dil-jale ki baar-e Khudaaya yeh aah thi

KHana KHaraab ho tera ai ishq be-hayaa
aaiin kaunsa tha yeh kya rasm-o-raah thi

tuune jo dil ko mere sanam-KHana kar diya
rehta Khuda tha jis meiN yeh voh baar-gaah thi

Tamkeen ko ik nigaah meiN divaana kar diya
jaadu-fareb aah yeh kis ki nigaah thi

Even the hellfire wanted refuge from it
This heavy sigh of a luckless soul burning in love

---

cure. All in all, a big load on the shoulders of one ghazal!

[128]'Kafir', in Arabic, means disbeliever or non-believer, one who rejects God (and therefore, as per Ghalib, someone who does not accord the status of Khuda to miyaan Auj). Mirza Ghalib delivers his praise in that sardonic-poetic manner he was famous for (and that is plainly evident in the Urdu original). In his vanity, however, miyaan Auj chooses to take the praise literally.

O terrible ishq, may you be destroyed
What law gave you this power, what tradition, which practice?

You have turned my heart into an idol house
Before this it used to be the abode of God

A single glance turned Tamkeen into a madman
How magical that was, whose eyes were those?

Everyone was full of appreciation for Tamkeen to give him encouragement. He was asked to read the last couplet again and again. Ustad Ehsaan said, 'Miyaan Yusuf! Excellent work! Keep at it and soon you will become an accomplished poet. But do consider taking on a teacher. Without an ustad, you might lose your way.'

Tamkeen replied with a smile, 'Ustad! How can I lose my way with your guidance? Tomorrow itself, inshallah, I will go to Ustad Auj.'

To this, Ustad Zauq added, 'Yes indeed, well-chosen! It's all settled then, in just a few weeks, you will become an expert.'

While these friendly comments were being exchanged, the second lamp was put before Ghulam Ahmad Tasveer. He is well known as miyaan Babban. He is unlettered and does not know the Urdu letter 'alif' from 'bay', but he has a great flair and passion for poetry. Earlier, he was miyaan Tanveer's shagird, but he later took Ustad Zauq as his teacher. He is heavily built, has a dark complexion, a small moustache and no beard. He's clothed in a simple attire of a narrow-bottomed cotton pyjama, kurta, a cotton kerchief draped over his shoulders and a handmade quilted cap on his head. He earns his living by doing hand-work on huqqa cords.

He's a talented poet in the truest sense because being unable to read and write, his verses arise spontaneously from his mind and heart. He has a phenomenal memory too. Much like an organ, once it is engaged, his memory faithfully records all that he says and hears. His poetry is simple and unaffected, and often inlaid with deeper meaning, so that even ustads are left shaking their heads in awe—hardly does it seem like an illiterate person's work. Let's just say that he is an excellent example of a divinely gifted poet. This is the ghazal he read:

hijr ki shab to sahar ho, ya rab
voh na aaya to qayamat hi sahi

jaan bekaar to apni na gayi
ai sitamgarh! teri shohrat hi sahi

mujh se itna bhi na kheNchiye saheb
aap par meri tabiyat hi sahi

jazbaa-e-dil nahiiN laaya tumko
aapki KHair inaayat hi sahi

Let the night of hijr become the dawn of meeting, O God!
Let the Day of Judgement come if she does not

My life was wasted but not for nothing
My tormentor, at least you came to be known

Don't take yourself away so far from me saheb!
Even if a one-sided attraction, let it be

You weren't pulled here by your heart's passion
Your kind favour is good enough for me.

At every sher, the listeners responded enthusiastically with an ovation of wah-wahs and Subhan-allah, until the gathering was ringing with exclamations.

When the ghazal concluded, Ustad Zauq turned to Hakim Momin Khan and remarked, 'Khan saheb, miyaan Babban is gifted in a unique way. He is supposed to be my shagird, but until now, I have not felt the need to make corrections in any sher that he has composed. He recited a ghazal yesterday that took me by surprise. One of the couplets came so naturally, I cannot praise it enough.' Turning to Babban, he asked, 'What was that sher, miyaan?'

Miyaan Babban could be seen applying pressure on his mind, and then, that gem of a couplet slipped down from his memory on to his tongue. Here is the matla of the ghazal Ustad Zauq referred to:

barchhi teri nigaah ki pehlu meiN aa lagi
pehlu se dil meiN dil se kaleje meiN jaa lagi

The dart of your glance, it pierced my side
From my side, it stabbed my heart and went still deeper inside.

The couplet that dazzled the ustad is this:

daaman pe voh rakkhe na rakkhe dilrubaa lagi
lekin hamaari KHaak THikaane se aa lagi

She is my sweetheart whether or not she holds me in her heart
My mortal dust has found its luminous home at last.

Hakim Momin Khan was moved and deeply appreciative. 'Miyaan Babban, truly this is God's gift to you; it is not born of any amount of learning. God bless you, you have made me profoundly happy today!'

After him, the lamp was taken to Muhammad Jafar Taabish. He belongs to Allahabad, but has been in the city of Dehli for many years. Although reclusive in temperament, he is fond of poetry and mushairas. He is sure to be seen at any mushaira that is held in the city. Two couplets in his ghazal were good, and those I'm reproducing here:

kabhi bin-baadaa reh nahiiN sakte
tauba kuchh hum ko saazkaar nahiiN

dil mein KHush haiN 'aduu paraaye, Taabish
voh sitamgar kisii ka yaar nahiiN

I cannot stay without my wine
To desist does not suit me

Rivals and strangers are pleased in their hearts, Taabish
My tyrannical beloved is nobody's friend for sure.

The last couplet gave such elegant closure that everyone spontaneously responded with loud wah-wahs. Mufti Sadruddin Aazurda was so mesmerised, he repeated the last couplet again and again.

After Taabish, the left side lamp came before Qalq. God save us from him, he's a cunning one! His name is Abdul Ali and he is from Madras. About thirty years old, he took off from his home town in early youth, coming to Dehli via Hyderabad. He is known to have trapped thousands in the hocus-pocus of charms and amulets, and for that reason, people are wary of him. He pretends to be holy, 'Shah Saheb', but who can tell about the real state of his heart? His poetry is quite good though. This is what he recited:

KHum-e sharaab se KHum-e garduN to ban gayaa
saqi banaa de maah pyaalaa uchhaal ke

hum mushraboN meiN chal ke, Qalq, mai-kashi karo
jhagDe vahaan nahiiN haiN haraam-o-halaal ke

The open mouth of the wine-jar reflects the heavens above
Put the moon on the sky, saqi, by tossing up the cup

O Qalq, drink in the tavern in the company of the like-minded

No feuds there on what's proscribed and what's permitted.

The lamp now moved to Munshi Mahmud Jan Auj.[129] In his ghazal there were only two couplets that got a little praise, the rest were mere fillers.

aane meiN us jaane-jaaN ke der hai
kuchh muqaddar ka hamare pher hai

hai yaqiin voh jaane-jaaN aata nahiiN
maut ke aane meiN phir kyuN der hai

There is delay in the arrival of my beloved
I believe it is to do with my turn of fate

I am certain my beloved is not going to come
But why too, is there a delay in the coming of death?

After him came the turn of Mirza Kamil Baig. He is a soldier and his pen name is 'Kamil'. He had come in uniform to the mushaira too. And what's more, he read his ghazal as if he were commanding a regiment. You will see how his ghazal has a militaristic hue as well. The qata[130] in his ghazal was most appealing though; here it is:

---

[129]Baig's original footnote: From now onwards, it is not necessary to explicitly state whether the right-hand lamp moves or the left-hand. Suffice it to know that a poet on the right side recites, and then a poet on the left side.

[130]Qata (also written as qita or qitaa') is derived from an Arabic root meaning 'to cut' or 'to cut off' and qata is, literally, a piece, a cutting, a segment or a detached piece. It is among the oldest and the longest surviving genres of Urdu poetry. While originally the qata was part of a qasidah or a ghazal, a self-contained piece that could also be read independently, it later established itself as an independent genre. Some began giving qata a title, and it became a kind of poem. A feature considered a must for a qata, as opposed to a ghazal, is the continuity of thought and presentation of a central theme in such a way that it consists of a proper beginning, middle and end.
https://www.dawn.com/news/970538/qata-an-old-and-delicate-genre-of-urdu-poetry

mizhgaaN se gar bache dil abru kare hai tukDe
yeh baat meine keh kar jab usse daad chaahi

kehne lage ke tarkash jis vaqt hove KHaali
talvaar phir na kheNche to kya kare sipaahi

If the heart escapes the torture of your lashes, your eyebrows slay me
When I said this and appealed for justice, she said

When the quiver is emptied of arrows, dear one,
What can the soldier do but brandish his sword?

Hakim Sayyad Muhammad Ta'ashshuq was next in line. He is about sixty-three or sixty-four years of age, and an eminently respected writer and physician, a well-rounded personality. But he expects even more of himself! He loves poetry and when he hears a good sher, he gets carried away and does not hesitate in the least to lavish accolades on the poet. The good man then expects that others will, in turn, praise him in the same manner and with the same generosity. He is not a bad poet, but to tell the truth, his shers don't also light up a mushaira such that listeners would be compelled to shower unstinted appreciation.

See for yourself, his ghazal:

tujh ko is meri aah-o-zaari par
rahm ai fitna-gar nahiiN aata

vaada-e shaam to kiya lekin
kuchh voh aata nazar nahiiN aata

tere biimaar ka hai yeh aalam
hosh do do pahar nahiiN aata

Have you no mercy for my piteous wails
O mischievous one!

She had promised to come in the evening
But there seems no sign of her coming

Such is the dejection of your lover
For hours together he doesn't come to his senses.

There was some lukewarm applause for his recitation, but it wasn't up to his expectation and he seemed disappointed at the end.

Now the lamp came to Mir Haseen Tajalli. The grandson of Mir Taqi Mir, he is sharp, highly intelligent and has a keen sense of humour. Mir saheb's unique insightfulness is reflected in his verse, as also his use of language. Tajalli's ghazal is usually short, but carries a lot of weight. And why not, he's the grandson of none other than the 'God of Urdu poetry'.[131]

miri vafaa pe tujhe roz shak tha, ai zaalim
yeh sar, yeh teG hai, le ab to aitbaar aaya

yeh shauq dekho pas-e-marg bhi Tajalli ne
kafan meiN khol di aakheN suna jo yaar aaya

You doubted my faithfulness every day, my tormentor!
Here's the sword and here's my head, now are you satisfied

What do you say of this passion, Tajalli, even in death
Opened his eyes in the shroud on hearing of the coming of the beloved.

---

[131]Mir Taqi Mir (1722–1810 CE), the most famous among pre-modern Urdu poets, is known as 'Khuda-e-sukhan'. He came to Delhi in or around 1733 CE from Agra, his birthplace, and made it his home. He returned to Agra in 1739 CE to get away from the savage invasion of Nadir Shah. In Agra, he fell in love with a married girl, and due to events that followed, had a mental breakdown that affected him deeply. Even after he returned to Delhi, and throughout his life, he continued to have recurring bouts of insanity. Mir Taqi Mir's poetry output is prodigious, and spans six divans, more than that of any other classical poet.

The second couplet was appreciated endlessly, and miyaan Tajalli looked eminently satisfied and pleased with himself.

After Tajalli, it fell to Hakim Sakhanand Raqam to read his ghazal. I had met him at Hakim Momin Khan saheb's house. His poetry is just about average, but his rendition is impressive. And while reading a ghazal, he acknowledges even the slightest praise with a string of salaams!

Here's his ghazal in this mushaira:

bujhana aatish-e-dil ka bhi kuchh haqiiqat hai
zaraa-sa kaam tujhe chashm-e-tar nahiiN aata

adam se kucha-e-qatil ki raah mulhaq hai
gayaa udhar jo guzar phir idhar nahiiN aata

ho KHaak chaaragari is mariiz ki tere
nazar meiN tujh-sa koi chaara-gar nahiiN aata

Putting out the fire of the heart is also real work
You don't even know how to do this, tear-filled eyes!

The lane to my beloved's house joins the road to oblivion
Whoever goes there never finds his way back

For this heartsick sufferer of yours, there's no cure
For I see no carer like you in sight.

The third sher was in the style of Hakim Momin Khan saheb's poetry, and expectedly, he gave much praise for it.[132] He also added, 'Miyaan Raqam! Either you remain a hakim and practice medicine, or you write poetry. This mixing up of the two is a difficult thing.'

Sheikh Niyaz Ahmad Josh was up next, and when the lamp

---

[132]Raqam was Momin Khan's pupil, and for his poetry to be influenced by his ustad's poetic sensibility was understandable, and indeed, something that both ustad and shagird took pride in.

reached him, all of Ustad Zauq's pupils sat up attentively. Josh is very dear to Ustad Zauq. He's only about eighteen or nineteen years old, but even so, has enormous creative talent. He is also hard working. His composing and understanding of poetry are much touted in the Qila. The ghazal he read at the mushaira, however, was not entirely to my taste. Of course, his friends from the Qila brought the house down with their cries of wah-wahs, and Ustad Zauq also motivated his pupil with a laudatory Subhan-allah, Subhan-allah.

See the ghazal, for I was possibly mistaken in my assessment:

kyuN kar voh haath aaye ki yaaN zor-o-zar nahiiN
le de ke ik aah so us meiN asar nahiiN

qismat se dard bhi to hua voh hameN nasiib
jis dard ka ke chaara nahiiN chaara-gar nahiiN

qismat hi meiN nahiiN hai shahaadat vagarna yaaN
voh zaKHm kaun-sa hai ke jo kaar-gar nahiiN

sajde meiN kyuN paDaa hai, are uTH sharaab pii
ai Josh! Mai-kadaa hai Khuda ka yeh ghar nahiiN

Why should she come to me when I have no power or wealth
In the end there's only a lovelorn sigh, that too, to no effect

It is my destiny that I had to have such a malady
That has no cure, and no healer

It is my fate that I should not become a martyr
Else what wound is it that causes no stir

Why are you in prayerful sajda, sit up, sip the wine
O Josh! This is a tavern, not the house of God divine.

And now, you've read the ghazal! I still maintain that I didn't find any couplet in it worthy of praise; it's another matter that people applauded just for the sake of it.

Now the lamp was brought up to Muhammad Abdul Aziz, the older son of Maulvi Imam Bakhsh Sehbai. His pen name is 'Aziz' and he composes fine ghazals. And why not, he is, after all, the son of a fine poet. He writes:

juN shama shaGl tere saraapa niyaaz ka
jalna jo soz ka hai, to rona gudaaz ka

kaj fahmiyoN se KHalq kii dekha ke kya hua
Mansur ko hariif na hona tha raaz ka

hum aasiyoN ka baar-e gunaah se jhuka hai sar
aur KHalq ko gumaan hai hum par namaaz ka

maGruur tha hi, aur voh maGruur ho gaya
is meiN gila nahiiN mujhe aaina-saaz ka

auroN ke saath lutf se tha surat-e-niyaaz
yaaN baDH gaya dimaaG taGaaful se naaz ka

The candle works to embody your entreaty sincere
The burning with passion, the softly melting with tears

See what the twisted minds of the world wrought
The secret of Mansur became his enemy fraught[133]

Sinners we are, heads bent with the burden of our sins
And the world imagines we are bowed in prayer

---

[133]This refers to Mansur al-Hallaj, a Sufi mystic and teacher during the Abbasid period. He is believed to have had a mystical revelation of God and unity with God, after which he said to his teacher, 'Ana al-haq! (I am the truth).' His teacher told him to keep his knowledge secret because nobody would understand its deeper essence. However, it was not to be, and the Abbasid caliph was enraged when he got to know of the utterance. Hallaj was executed on the charge of heresy.

She was arrogant, and became more arrogant still
But I have no complaint of the mirror maker[134]

With others, there was the appearance of being humble
When I was indifferent, it made her haughty and proud.

Now tell me, isn't the entire ghazal studded with gems? I agree that for this ghazal, all praise was well deserved. Ustad Zauq also conceded. 'Bhai Sehbai, your son has tremendous talent, may God enhance his life. One day, he will be a famous man.' Turning to Aziz, he said, 'Wah sahebzade, wah! What a heart-warming performance! Indeed, a great father and an accomplished son!'

Miyaan Aziz got up and bowed respectfully to acknowledge the ustad's compliments.

After miyaan Aziz, Khwaja Muinuddin Yakta was next in line. What should I say of him? He was bestowed the title of 'Khan' by the government and now he thinks nobody is his equal. He becomes a shagird of some teacher, then goes on to some other teacher. Sometime back, Ehsaan was his teacher, now he has drifted to Mirza Ghalib. Such a fickle-minded person, he will never learn anything! Nobody praised him for his ghazal, and I don't hesitate to admit that I was rather pleased about that. He would have resented that, for sure. But then, who would praise shers like these:

ai aah-e-shola za! Yeh KHas-o-KHaar bhi nahiiN
nau aasmaan haiN, do bhi nahiiN, chaar bhi nahiiN

hai kisko taab-e-shikva-e-dushman ke zo'f se
lab par hamare tazkirah-e yaar bhi nahiiN

---

[134]The mirror or the act of 'mirroring' (as in water) is an elegantly familiar motif in Urdu poetry, and in its orbit are ideas of the craftsman or mirror-maker (alluding to God), looking into the mirror as a way of self-realisation, reflections (of one's face or character or emotions) and the fleeting, ephemeral nature of creation itself.

jiina firaaq-e-yaar meiN vaade ki laag par
aasaan gar nahiiN hai to dushvaar bhi nahiiN

O burning sighs! These are not dried grass or twigs
There are nine heavens to burn, not two or four

Who has the energy to fret and fume at the enemy
When even the beloved's praise is not on my lips

To live in separation from the beloved on her slender promise
Is not easy for sure but not so difficult either.

Yes, now the lamp moves to a person who is a real poet. Who is he? He is Mirza Haji Beg Shohrat. About thirty to thirty-two years old, with a fair complexion and of medium height, he is always well groomed. He used to host a mushaira at his home until some time ago; now it has been discontinued. He is a star pupil of Mufti Sadruddin Aazurda. Not only does he write well, but he also recites his ghazal in an engaging manner, in a ringing gravelly voice. When he recites, he enunciates each word such that it seeps into the soil of the heart. Every sher of his ghazal was praised, as it ought to have been. This is the ghazal:

ek din, do din, kahaaN tak, tu bhi kuchh insaaf kar
yeh to jalna roz kaa, ai soz-e-hijraaN ho gaya

hai taraqqi jauhar-e-qaabil hi ke shaayaaN ke maiN
KHaak ka putla banaa, putle se insaaN ho gaya

kufr-o-diiN meiN thaa na kuchh uqda ba-juz band-e-naqaab
uske khulte hi yeh kaar-e-mushkil aasaaN ho gaya

pehle da'va-e-KHudai us but-e-kaafir ko tha
kuchh durusti par jo aaj aaya to insaaN ho gaya

One day, two days, until when... I plead for justice
This burning every day is like the pain of estrangement

> It's the stone with essence that's chiselled into a gem, and I
> Was fashioned from dust into a clay figure, then became human
>
> Adoration of the beloved was not difficult, except there remained a veil
> The moment the veil lifted, everything became clear
>
> Earlier this worshipper of the beloved had a notion of the divine
> Today when he has come to his senses, he's become human.

On the last sher, Mirza Ghalib was in a state of enchantment. He slapped his thigh and cried out, 'Wah, miyaan Shohrat, wah! This is remarkable! It's not a sher, it's a miracle! This one couplet can take on even the greatest of divans, what a sher! Subhan-allah!

> Earlier this worshipper of the beloved had a notion of the divine
> Today when he has come to his senses, he's become human.'

He repeated the last sher yet again to soak in the emotion. The ghazal created an electric atmosphere. People were repeating the ghazal to themselves, or reciting it to those beside them to dive deeper into its coruscating depths. Calls of wah-wahs and Subhan-allah filled the cooling night air, and it was some time before the mehfil had some order and silence.

The lamp now came to Nawazish Haseen Khan Tanveer. A young man of thirty-two or thirty-three years, he is much favoured by Badshah Salamat. After Shohrat's ghazal that had infused joyous energy in the listeners, nobody paid much attention to Tanveer's ghazal. It was an ordinary piece too, and only this qata was of note:

jaan kar dil meiN mujhe apna mariiz-e-tap-e-Gam
kehta logoN se ba-zahir but-e ayyar hai kya

rang-e-ruKH zard hai, tar chashm hai, lab par dam-e-sard
puchhna isse ke is shaKHs ko aazaar hai kya

Even when she knows in her heart my torment for her
The artful beloved asks people aloud

He has a pale face, tearful eyes and a cold sigh on his lips
Ask this man what affliction he suffers from.

After him, it was the turn of Mir Bahadur Ali Hazeen, serious, sober and particularly dignified. He is Arif's shagird. Of his ghazal, one couplet was creditable.

sabu se muNh lagaenge ab itna sabr hai kisko
ke bharye KHum se mai shiishe meiN aur shiishe se saaGar meiN

I will drink directly from the wine pitcher, who has the patience now
To pour from the pitcher into the glass ewer, and from the ewer into the wine cup?

The interesting shers of the ghazal that he recited are these:

duniya ki vus'atein tere goshe meiN aa gayiN
Allah re! vus'atein tiri ai tangnaae dil

jal-jal ke aaKHirash tapish-e-Gam ke haath se
ek daaG rah gayaa mire pehlu meiN, jaaye dil

dekha voh apni aaNkh se jo kuchh sunaa na tha
aur dekhiye Hazeen abhi kya kya dikhaaye dil

Your little corner has become my entire world
Allah re! How wide is the strait of your heart

I have been burning in the flame of your sorrow, in the end
Only a scar remains in my side where once my heart had been

I saw with my own eyes what I had never heard of
Let's see, Hazeen, what more the heart has to show.

Everyone especially appreciated the maqta, and indeed, it is very good.

After him, the lamp came to a person who is himself a poet, whose father is a poet, whose older brother is a poet and whose entire family are poets. And who is that? He is miyaan Baqar Ali Jafri. He is Fakhr-ush-Shora Nizamuddin Mamnuun's younger brother, and Malik-ush-Shora Qamar-ud-Din Minnat's younger son.[135] Now, if his ghazal won't be packed with a punch, whose will be? Here are two couplets from the ghazal he recited at the mushaira:

teG yuN dil meiN khayaal-e-yaar na kheNch
na-Khuda taras! tu Kaa'be meiN to talvaar na kheNch

be-sar-o-paa chaman-o-dasht meiN aalam ke na phir
naaz-e-har gul na uTHa, minnat-e-har KHaar na kheNch

Don't wound the heart thus with the beloved's thought-sword
Godless one! In the Holy Kaa'ba don't brandish your sword

Don't go unprotected into the gardens and wilderness
Indulge not every flower's vanity, don't fret about removing each thorn.

---

[135]Fakhr-ush-Shora or Pride and Jewel of Poets; Malik-ush-Shora or Chief Poet of the State.

The ghazal was not accorded the appreciation it merited. The reason is that poetry of this style is now fading from Dehli. There is now excessive focus on the mundane, and if a theme is born of or dabbles in the everydayness of life, it is greatly appreciated. Mirza Ghalib used to be partial to the traditional themes, but sadly, he too seems to be turning his back on those now.

After this, it was the turn of Munshi Muhammad Ali Tishna. The chobdaar hesitated to put the lamp before him. There he sat on folded legs, swaying with his eyes shut, enjoying the ghazals being recited and, of course, naked as he had been when he'd come. The chobdaar hung back and looked towards Mirza Fakhru, who signalled that he should go ahead, and finally, the chobdaar placed the lamp in front of Tishna. As the light hit his face, miyaan Tishna opened his eyes. A thought crossed his mind and he bent forward to blow out the light. Then he announced, 'I would also like to recite something!' Everyone replied, 'Please go ahead!'

He recited this ghazal in his free-flowing and unencumbered style, singing it and reciting it in parts.

aaNkh paDti hai kahiiN, paanv kahiiN paDta hai
sab ki hai tumko KHabar, apni KHabar kuchh bhi nahiiN

shama hai, gul bhi hai, bulbul bhi hai, parvanaa bhi
raat ki raat yeh sab kuchh hai, sehar kuchh bhi nahiiN

hashr ki dhuum hai, sab kehte haiN yuN hai yuN hai
fitna hai ik tiri THokar ka, magar kuchh bhi nahiiN

nestii ki hai mujhe kucha-e-hasti meiN talaash
sair karta huuN udhar ki ke jidhar kuchh bhi nahiiN

ek aaNsu bhi asar jab na kare, ai Tishna
faaeda rone se, ai diida-e-tar, kuchh bhi nahiiN

The eyes land somewhere, somewhere else land the feet
You know of everyone else, but of yourself, you know nothing

There's the lamp, the rose, the nightingale, and all its admirers
Tonight there's all this, in the morning all is gone, there's nothing

The Day of Judgement is much talked of, everyone says it's like this or that
It's only the trickery of being tripped by You, else it is nothing

My search is for non-existence in the lanes of being
I roam in places where there is nothing

When a single sorrowful tear has no effect, O Tishna!
No use shedding copious streams, it means nothing.

What should I tell you of the reaction this ghazal produced! A deep and dark stillness swept up and seemed to shroud everything. The theme of the ghazal, the spell of the midnight hour, the state of the poet delivering the ghazal—it all touched a chord with everyone, and at the end of it, the whole mehfil seemed bewitched. Here, the audience was in this frame, and there, miyaan Tishna was seen walking out of the door still lost in his own world, throwing up his hands and saying to himself, again and again, 'Kuchh bhi nahiiN, there is nothing!' His words lingered behind long after he had gone, echoing in everyone's head. When people awoke from their reverie, everyone could only utter the phrase, as if on cue. 'Indeed, there *is* nothing!'[136]

---

[136]The poignancy in this ghazal is the clearest mirror yet of the mood among the elite of the time. The poets were well aware of how fragile the veneer of their days was, and how it was a matter of time before it might be lost forever. *'Tonight there's all this, in the morning all is gone, there's nothing…'*.

Mirza Fakhru brought everyone's attention back. He summoned for the extinguished lamp and lit it again. 'Kind sirs! Please get started once more!'

The lamp was now taken to Hafiz Muhammad Hussain Bismil. But after Tishna, how was it possible for Bismil to make any impact? First of all, he lacks experience; he's a pupil of Mirza Qadir Bakhsh Sabir. And then, his ghazal also did not have anything special, although the maqta was good. Here is the ghazal:

dil tu ne hamse O but-e-kafir uTHa liya
is nazuki pe bojh yeh kyuN kar uTHa liya

baar-e garaan-e ishq falak se na uTH sakaa
kya jaane mere dil ne yeh kyuN kar uTHa liya

piir-e-muGaaN ne Bismil mai-kash ko dekh kar
shiisha baGal meiN, haath meiN saGar uTHa liya

You have taken away my heart from me, O beloved
How will you bear its burden, delicate as you are

When heaven is unable to endure the weight of ishq
My heart! How did you think of containing it

When the tavern-keeper caught sight of Bismil the drunkard
He tucked the flask at his side and took away the glass.

Some listened with attention, some did not; the ghazal received scant praise, and the lamp now moved to Mir Husain Taskeen. He is about forty years of age, and is Sehbai's shagird. He has also obtained islah from Hakim Momin Khan for some time. His family is well known in Dehli. It was his grandfather, Mir Haider, who had killed Mir Hussain Ali, Farrukhsiyar's prime minister.[137]

---

[137]Farrukhsiyar was one of the later Mughals (1713–19 CE), in whose reign the EIC obtained duty-free trading rights in Bengal against an annual payment of three

Taskeen is a soldier and a fairly good poet too. He goes:

hazaar tarah se karni paDi tasalli-e-dil
kisii ke jaane se go KHud nahiiN qaraar mujhe

shab-e-visaal meiN sunanaa paDa fasaana-e-Gair
samajhte kaash na apna voh raazdaar mujhe

mere qusur se diidaar meiN hui taaKHiir
na dekhna tha tamasha-e-rozgaar mujhe

maze yeh dekhe haiN aaGaaz-e-ishq meiN Taskeen
ke sujhta nahiiN apna maa'al-e-kaar mujhe

I had to comfort the heart in a thousand different ways
As if I was myself distraught at somebody's leaving

On the night of our meeting, I had to hear stories of my rival
If only she did not regard me as her trusted friend

The blame is mine, seeing my beloved was delayed
In the tamasha of life, I should never have got waylaid

What delights I have known Taskeen, in the first flush of love
That now, I am unable to see the purpose of my days.

This ghazal struck the right note and changed the mood of the gathering, so that everyone again became alert and animated. The lamp now came to Khwaja Ghulam Husain Bedil, shagird of Ustad Ehsaan. He read this ghazal:

nigah ki, chashm ki, zulf-e dotaa ki
sahe ik dil jafaa kis kis balaa ki

---

thousand rupees; this was in 1717 CE. The town of Farrukhnagar in Gurgaon, south of Delhi, has been named after him.

kab us gul ki gali tak jaa sake hai
hava baandhii hai yaaroN ne havva ki

butoN se milte ho raatoN ko Bedil
tumheN bhi din lage qudrat Khuda ki

Your eyes, your glance, the braid of your hair
What all manner of tyranny can the heart bear

When could I go to the lane of that beauty
Whom friends have made famous everywhere

Bedil you have started meeting beauties at night
You are taking your time! Good heavens!

The ghazal was wishy-washy; who would have given praise for this? On the other hand, Muhammad Hussain Ta'ib's ghazal that came after this was immensely moving. Ta'ib is the nephew of Maulana Shah Abdul Aziz Dehlvi, the well-known hadith scholar. Also, he is the pupil of Fakhr-ush-Shora Nizamuddin Mamnuun. In a short metre, Ta'ib wove such an outstanding ghazal! Subhan-allah! And his recitation is beyond all words of praise. This was his ghazal:

phir kataan-vaar[138] *jigar chaak hua*
phir koi maah-laqaa yaad aaya

kahiye us but ko mushaabah kis ke
dekh kar jis ko Khuda yaad aaya

ahd-e piirii meiN javaani ki umang
aah! kis vaqt meiN kya yaad aaya

[138]The kataan silk is fabled to be so fine and delicate that it can be rent by moonlight. Today, kataan silk is a heritage fabric of Bangladesh and exquisite wedding sarees are woven from it. Kataan silk has also made the gorgeous Benarasi sarees, in many lustrous varieties, renowned all over the world.

Again the silken heart was shredded to pieces
Again I remembered my moon-faced beloved

To whom should I compare that peerless beauty
When I look at her, I remember the Almighty

In my old age I feel the eagerness of youth
Ah! What a time to have what a thought!

On the second and third couplets, people kept showering accolades and miyaan Ta'ib got tired of acknowledging them with salaam after salaam. When the euphoria subsided somewhat, the lamp moved to Ustad Zauq's teacher, Ustad Ghulam Rasool Shauq.[139] He is an old man, and used to be Shah Nasir's shagird. He is also the imam at the Azizabadi Masjid. In the days gone by, Zauq took his kalaam for islah to him. Due to that old association, Shauq still considers himself to be the teacher and wants Zauq to still reach out for revisions. I felt he looked a bit senile. The opening sher of his ghazal, the matla, was quite impactful. As for the rest of the ghazal, thank God, it got over quickly!

likhaa hua hai yeh us maah-jabiiN ke parde par
nahiiN hai koi ab aisa zamiiN ke parde par

It's written on the veil of that moon-like beauty
There's no one like her now on the screen of the earth.

All the master poets, Ghalib, Momin Khan, Aazurda, Sehbai were full of praise for miyaan Shauq's ghazal, with enthusiastic calls of wah-wahs. The appreciation was not for the ghazal, it was to needle Ustad Zauq. Zauq understood of course.[140]

[139]Hafiz Ghulam Rasool was a Quran reciter who lived near Zauq's house. He wrote poetry under the pen name 'Shauq'.

[140]Zauq and the other ustads were bound in a relationship of bitter-sweet rivalry, with non-fatal word-bouts being commonplace, not only to their own mutual satisfaction, but also to the amused delight of all of Delhi. Ghalib and Zauq had

Miyaan Shauq, however, didn't quite see through it; he thought it was genuine commendation of his ghazal and was pleased. He turned towards Ustad Zauq and remarked, 'See, this is how shers are written!'

Zauq only smiled and remained silent out of courtesy towards his old teacher. One or two of his pupils tried to respond on Zauq's behalf, but Zauq did not let them.

In due course, the hullabaloo settled and the lamp continued to the poet next in line, Azad. His real name is Alexander Heatherly and he is French.[141] He was born and raised in Dehli and has received all his education here. It was from Dehli that he became a captain in the army and went to Alwar. He is about twenty-one years old and is well-versed in medicine. He is also passionate about poetry and is Arif's shagird. When he heard about the mushaira, he immediately presented himself at Dehli. His attire is military, but he speaks in Urdu, and such chaste Urdu too, as if a Dehli-wallah is speaking![142] His shers are good as well; I think it is remarkable that a Frenchman should recite such poetry. This is his ghazal:

voh garm ruuh-e raah-e ma'asi hoN jahaaN meiN
garmi se rahaa naam na daaman meiN tarii ka

---

an openly scrappy relationship. Nonetheless, they were literary contemporaries, children of a tehzeeb they could see fading before their eyes, something that pained them both in equal measure.

[141]Farhatullah Baig is mistaken about Azad's French ancestry and his name, spelling it as 'Headlay'. Alexander Heatherly's father was English and his mother Indian. He was Arif's pupil and used 'Azad' or 'Alec' as his pen name. Akhtar Qamber (trans), *The Last Musha'irah of Dehli*, Endnote 47, pp. 165–66.

[142]This is Farhatullah Baig's typical style of humour—understated and good-natured. Azad was indeed a complete 'Dehli-wallah', as the reader can see. So, this seems less like an allusion to Azad's foreign ancestry and more of an attempt to poke fun at the-then typical Dehli-wallah's provincial attitude, especially in matters relating to Urdu adab and poetry.

kuchh paaoN meiN taaqat ho to kar dasht navardii
haathoN se mazaa dekh zaraa jeb-darii ka

chehlum ko ayaadat ke liye voh meri aaye
Azad! THikana bhi hai is beKHabrii ka

When I set foot on the hot twisted road of the world
The heat leaves no trace of moistness in my shirt

If your feet have vigour, go wandering in the desert
Know the madness of your hands tearing off your shirt

She came to ask about my wellbeing at my chehlum[143]
Azad! Is there any limit to her indifference!

After Azad, the lamp came to the other side, to Mir Shuja'at Ali Tasalli. He is poor and old, about sixty-four or sixty-five years of age, and was dressed in ordinary, worn-out clothes. He is a much-loved shagird of Shah Nasir. He was considered the 'Jur'at' of his time.[144] But for some time now, he has withdrawn from the world and become a recluse, preferring to spend his days at the Qadam Shareef.[145] There are still times, however, when the

[143]Chehlum is the fortieth day of mourning in the family after someone's death.

[144]About the actual poet Jur'at: He was known as Sheikh Qalandar Bakhsh, and his real name was Yaḥya Amaan. He was born in Delhi, but spent his childhood in Faizabad and then migrated to Lucknow. He was a close friend of Insha Allah Khan 'Insha', one of the well-known rekhti poets, and a regular at the court of Sulaiman Shikoh. He lost his eyesight in the prime of his youth, but still wrote poetry and was passionate about music and astrology. He died in Lucknow in 1809. He has been included in Azad's literary canon in *Aab-e hayat*, as a rekhti poet of the fourth era.

[145]The Dargah Qadam Shareef in Paharganj consists of a tomb complex built by Firoz Shah Tughlaq (1309–1388 CE), containing a mosque, a madrasa and a shrine, and surrounded by a massive gated wall. Originally, Firoz Shah built it for himself, but when his son Fateh Khan died in 1376 CE, he was buried there. It is called the 'Qadam Shareef' because of a precious relic—a stone slab with the footprint of the Prophet Muhammad—that stands prominently above Fateh Khan's grave. It is

magnet of a mushaira pulls him towards the lights of Dehli. His style of recitation is quite unique—like a conversation between two persons. When you see the ghazal, you will feel like a lover is talking with his beloved.

kaisi THokar jaDi hai hazrat-e dil
paaoN par uske sar dharo to sahi

jab kahaa meine tum pe marta huuN
tum gale se mere lago to sahi

bole voh kya maze ki baateN haiN
KHair hai kuchh, pare haTo to sahi

Gair ki kal voh lag ke chhaati se
mujh se kehne lage suno to sahi

is liye uske hum gale se lage
ke zaraa jii meiN tum jalo to sahi

How you have made me stumble, dear heart!
Now place your head at her feet

When I said to her, I die for you
Let me hold you at least

She said, these are nice things to say
Whatever it is, give way at least

---

said to have been brought from Mecca by Firoz Shah's spiritual guide and teacher.

The dargah also features in an intriguing story about Aurangzeb, from about three centuries later. After overthrowing and imprisoning his father Shah Jahan and disposing of his brothers, Aurangzeb wanted to make his accession to the grand Mughal throne in 1658 CE an event to remember. In particular, he wanted to demonstrate his brand of tough, uncompromising justice. So, he stood and executed 500 thieves before the walls of this dargah. This event left a deep and lasting impression on Niccolo Manucci, long-standing Venetian physician at the Mughal court, and he duly recorded it.

Yesterday she was in the arms of a stranger
When she said, 'listen to me...

The reason I embraced the stranger was
So you'd eat your heart out at least.'

This ghazal did not get the praise it should have because now had come the time when sleep was beginning to overpower everyone, heads were starting to spin and the faculty to discern between good and bad had become foggy. After this, a couple of ghazals were recited, and they were all received in a similar lacklustre manner; nobody really listened, and it was all quite colourless.

After Tasalli, Shor read his ghazal. He is from Kol[146] and is Christian by faith. His name is George Puech, and it's not known whose pupil he is. He keeps visiting Dehli from time to time though. What he writes is good enough![147]

aajiz tha apni jaan se aisa tira mariiz
dekhe se jiske haalat-e Isa tabaah thi

balbe yeh beKHudi ke KHudi se bhula diya
varna yeh ziist marg ki apni gavaah thi

dair-o-haram meiN to na de tarjiih zaahida
jis simt sar jhuka vahi bas sajda-gaah thi

---

[146]Kol is a village near Aligarh in Uttar Pradesh.

[147]George Puech 'Shor' (1823–1894), whose pen name means noise, wrote six volumes of Urdu poetry, a Persian divan and an anthology of religious poems. He was of French descent and the maternal grandson of Francois Koine 'Farasu', from whom he imbibed his love for Urdu poetry. Puech's descendants, George Puech Jr. and Maurice Puech resided in Meerut until the mid- to late-twentieth century.

George Puech was one of the Francisis, families of French, Dutch, Armenian, Portuguese, German and British descent who came to be termed as such in the eighteenth and nineteenth centuries. The term was in use right up to the second decade of the twentieth century when the last of the prominent Armenians died in Agra. *https://www.thehindu.com/features/metroplus/The-story-of-the-Francisis/article15783761.ece*

So powerless was your sufferer for his life
To see him would have destroyed Jesus Christ

I became aloof from life with utterances of losing my self
Else this life would have been witness to my death

Have no preference, devout one, for mosque or temple
Whichever place you bow your head is a place of worship.

After him it was the turn of Muhammad Askari Naalaan. But in that state of sleepy stupor, who could be expected to hear the voice of this ninety-year-old poet or listen to the recitation of his ghazal? He is Ustad Mushafi's first pupil; now of course, he is a relic of olden times. His poetry is also of a bygone era.

sahar ke hone ka dil ko khayaal rehta hai
shab-e-visaal bhi dil ko malaal rehta hai

voh bad-gumaaN hoN ke us but ke saaye par bhi mujhe
raqiib hi ka sadaa ehtemaal rehta hai

The heart is ever mindful of the approach of dawn
Even through the night of our meeting it remains fearful

She is not to be trusted and even for her shadow
I apprehend my rival has designs on her.

And now after miyaan Naalaan, the lamp reached Meer saheb. Instantly, everyone perked up with renewed interest and vigour. Some were seen rubbing their eyes with their fingers, others used the hem of their kurta to soak the sleep out of their eyes, and still others went to all the trouble of going out, splashing water on their faces before resuming their seats. Anything to ward off the waves of slumber that threatened to throw cold water on the brilliance of the upcoming performance. The prospect of Meer saheb's recitation awakened everybody instantaneously. Mirza Fakhru had been leaning on one side until then, now he leaned the other way for a fresh perspective. A smile crossed the faces of the ustads and young people began to exchange excited whispers. Meer saheb, on his part, rose and came ahead of his seat.

Mirza Fakhru said, 'Meer saheb, this is not good enough! You need to come right to the centre and read your ghazal.'

Mirza Fakhru gave an imperceptible signal and the chobdaar picked up both the lamps and placed them in the centre of the courtyard. Meer saheb took the cue and proceeded to seat himself right in front of the shamiana.

Is there anyone at all in Dehli who does not know Meer saheb? Is there any mushaira that he does not add sparkle to? Is there any mehfil that his benign presence does not enrich? There must be only a handful of people who might know his real name; I have always known his name to be Meer saheb. He is about seventy years old, tall and gaunt in build. He has a fair complexion, drooping eyes, a parrot-like hooked nose and a broad jawline with a long beard. His head is round and he has sparse, short hair.

He is well loved and recognised throughout the city, and even a child will be able to describe him to you, his sparkling clean clothes, a white single-width pyjama with a matching white kurta, and on top of it, a white angrakha. Not to forget the arqcheen cap covering his head. He has a thoughtful and serious look on his face, but when he loses his temper, he is quite beyond anyone's control. Even so, regardless of their age, everyone had an easy relationship with him, exchanging light-hearted pleasantries and jokes, to which Meer saheb would respond fitfully, often giving back measure for measure, so as to leave the other person speechless. He did not care then whether his response was relevant or if it made any sense.

At a mushaira, everybody loved to joke with him, from the youthful Tamkeen to Badshah Salamat himself; on his part, Meer saheb did not mind either one's ribbing. He did not also rein himself in while making a riposte, whether to Tamkeen or to the Emperor. He would recite his ghazal extempore as per the occasion, and could not be bothered with writing it out beforehand. In his ghazals, he felt no need to follow the rules of grammar and balance, and deigned only to respect the rhyming schemes of radiif and qafiya.

Whatever he wished to narrate, he would express in prose, comfortably and at length. Even as he was reciting, someone would interrupt with an objection and he would patiently respond to it. Eventually, however, when he grew tired of speaking and replying to objectors, he would bring it to a quick close with the incorporation of the radiif and qafiya. Usually when he started reciting, almost instantly there would be a flurry of objections. Meer saheb was not easy to faze; he would face all objections squarely and keep up the good fight! When his words were not enough to subdue the objector, he would rise from his seat in hot-headed agitation. When this happened, somebody or the other from the audience got him to take his seat again, suitably reprimanded the objector and at the same time, mollified Meer saheb until finally peace was regained. Thereafter, the whole process would start all over again, with another irksome detractor rising to needle our Meer saheb.

Mamluk-ul Ali especially got a kick out of getting into verbal entanglements with Meer saheb. And on his part, Meer saheb would engage lustily, giving back eye for eye. In fact, their arguments were such that if any of Mamluk-ul Ali's students had watched them unfold, all his authority and clout at the madrasa would have bowed out of the door.

As Meer saheb sat in front of the lamp,[148] he cast his gaze over

[148]Baig's original footnote: Meer saheb died after the 1857 Uprising. Miyaan Kaale saheb's son, miyaan Nizamuddin used to hold mushairas at his house that were attended by Meer saheb. Others who attended those same mushairas are still to be found in Dehli, and it is from them that I (Farhatullah Baig) came to know of Meer

the gathering and began. 'Hazrat, today I will recite a qasidah[149] in praise of Hudhud. He is a great one to sing his own praises. Today, he will have to listen attentively to a hajv in his honour.'[150]

Everyone dislikes Hudhud intensely, and now when they heard that a hajv was on the cards, and that too by Meer saheb, they enthusiastically responded, 'Yes, Meer saheb. Please go ahead.'

Miyaan Hudhud was a minion of Hakim Aaga Jaan Aish and strutted about thanks to the latter's favour and protection. It was now Hakim Aaga Jaan's turn to feel the heat therefore, when he heard that Meer saheb had prepared a hajv for his pet. He got concerned that he too might get pulled into the story. Also, if someone else other than Meer saheb had chosen to recite a hajv, one could reply to it, satire for satire; but who on earth could manage a response to Meer saheb's bahr-e-taviil, those long-winding narratives?[151]

---

saheb and his style and have recorded the same. He has not been mentioned in any tazkirah, and that's possibly because he was not seen as a serious poet of that era.

[149]From the early tradition, a qasidah is not simply an ode, but a poem with a purpose (maqsad).

[150]Hajv or satire is a poem of humorous insult or abuse; some poems in this genre are light-hearted and witty, others genuinely nasty; some scatological or obscene. Mirza Mohammad Rafi Sauda was famous for this form, and Mir Taqi Mir speaks of him composing a 'qasidah dar hajv', a qasidah of satire. Traditionally, praise and insult, ode and satire were two sides of the same literary coin.

In later years, when Victorian morality took Urdu poetry under its wing and began to enforce its strict codes of literary correctness, this genre was especially slammed and criticised. Frances W. Pritchett, *Nets of Awareness: Urdu Poetry and its Critics*, p. 170.

[151]Bahr-e-taviil is an exceedingly long metre in Urdu, Persian and Arabic verse; one line or misra of a two-line verse can be longer than a full ghazal. It can be understood as Urdu rap, with its rhythm and cadence. Watch this video to enjoy the breeze flowing through the recitation of a bahr-e-taviil by Dr Azra Raza, co-author of *Ghalib: Epistemologies of Elegance*. She is also Professor of Medicine at Columbia University, New York. *https://www.youtube.com/watch?v=f0tnP_2xk9U*

At a loss, Hakim Aaga Jaan bundled off Hudhud by hiding him behind the gao-takiyas and then literally made him vanish from the gathering. Now when Meer saheb looked in that direction, Hudhud was gone! Meer saheb was astonished; he looked this way and then that way in bewilderment, but Hudhud was nowhere to be seen. Meer saheb was nonplussed for a few moments, and then he announced to the mehfil, 'I will now postpone the hajv and read a ghazal in its place.'

Everyone entreated him. 'Why Meer saheb? Why have you changed your mind? Read the hajv, Meer saheb, for God's sake read it! After Sauda, the hajv retreated completely from Urdu poetry. If you too don't give it any attention, then it will be the end. The garden of Urdu language will forever remain incomplete.'

Meer saheb was firm in his refusal, 'No sirs! If Hudhud were present, I would have said what I had to, to his face. To say it in his absence is not a hajv, but stabbing him in the back. I despise such people who stab others in the back and I will not do so myself.'

When he saw Meer saheb take such a stand, Hakim Aaga Jaan breathed a deep sigh of relief. He eagerly chimed in with some well-chosen words on the difference between reciting a hajv to the face of the protagonist and doing so behind his back. And thus was averted a poetic crisis with God's invisible help.

And now that the matter of the hajv was put to rest, Meer saheb began his ghazal. Only God knows what he recited. What everyone understood was only that the qafiya was 'teer', 'peer', 'kheer' and the radiif was 'hai'. Apart from this rather simple fact, forget about my understanding, I doubt if Meer saheb himself also fully knew what he was reciting and what the mazmuun of his ghazal was. It was all gloriously vague. Of course, when the qafiya and the radiif were spotted, people knew it had drawn to its close and began showering praise on him. Someone half-heartedly raised a flimsy objection, and sure enough, the instant it was voiced,

Meer saheb flew into one of his famous rages. This was what everyone was waiting for; his outrage was entertaining for everyone, the lighter side of the mushaira. Go ahead, see for yourself, the objections and Meer saheb's endearingly whimsical reactions!

As he was reciting the ghazal, Meer saheb stretched one line or misra, and stretched it so much that it went on and on, with no end in sight. Maulvi Mamluk-ul Ali remarked, 'Aji Meer saheb, this misra has landed in the zone of a bahr-e-taviil!'

Meer saheb irritably retorted, 'Maulvi saheb, have you ever seen a bahr-e-taviil? Or have you objected only on the basis of what you might have heard from here and there? First read *Mutawwal*... you should go and read *Mutawwal*, then you will know what exactly a bahr-e-taviil is.'

Mamluk-ul Ali sat there befuddled at Meer saheb's response. He persisted, 'Meer saheb, but what is the connection between *Mutawwal* and bahr-e-taviil? It's like saying, "I hit my knee and lost my eye!" You are just saying whatever comes to your head!'

Meer saheb now felt the need for a sympathiser, someone to back him, and he threw a glance towards Maulana Sehbai. Maulana Sehbai rose to the occasion and went along with Meer saheb's version of *Mutawwal*. Without showing disrespect to either party, he turned to Mamluk-ul Ali and gently chided him, 'Maulvi saheb, if the *Mutawwal* is not written in a bahr-e-taviil, then what is it? Are you now trying to cow down our good Meer saheb with the weight of your scholarship?'

This was all the reinforcement Meer saheb needed. Now he was a lion, and away he went, rampaging through the brush of intellect and knowledge he probably didn't know half as well as the learned teacher Mamluk-ul Ali.[152]

---

[152]Meer saheb is an intriguing figure. He is evidently a version of the quintessential comic relief, but he is also someone who is loved by one and all for his simple and straightforward manner. On the other hand, Meer saheb does not hesitate to spin tall stories about his knowledge and grasp of subjects. This facet of his is well

Neatly dovetailing into Sehbai's light-hearted comment to Mamluk-ul Ali, Meer saheb went on in a serious vein, 'Yes, Maulvi saheb, you must think that except you, nobody at all has read *Mutawwal*, right? Hazrat! I go through it twice every day. Yesterday, I sat down to write a ghazal in one of its metres, and I got tired of all the writing it needed. One misra extended over a hundred and seventy-five pages. I had to stop only because the pages in the notebook got exhausted. Otherwise, only God knows how much the line would have extended.'

It was now Mirza Nausha's turn to speak up. He said, 'Meer saheb, what you say is absolutely true. Our Maulvi Mamluk-ul Ali has really not seen a bahr-e-taviil. Ask me, my nephew Khwaja Amaan, do you know him? He has written a book, *Bostan-e Khayaal*. It is this big and fat!' With both his hands outstretched, Mirza Nausha indicated the impressive dimensions of his nephew's book. He continued, 'It is in twelve volumes and written in a bahr-e-taviil, so that the volumes are composed of only twelve lines. Your misra, Meer saheb, is not in a bahr-e-taviil but in the metre of a rubai actually.'

Meer saheb snorted loudly and shot back. 'Wah Mirza saheb! You were walking straight, then you too lost your way! Do you even know the metres of a rubai? Just tell me which book contains them?'

This was, yet again, a strange question, and Mirza Ghalib quickly retreated into the safety of silence. Meer saheb helpfully answered his own question. 'I knew your objection was not genuine, you simply objected for the fun of it! Mirza saheb, *Arba'een* is what

---

known to his peers, so teachers like Mamluk-ul Ali and Mirza Ghalib are seen to interject, but they also desist from seriously pursuing their line of objection. In the end, Meer saheb has the last word and nobody minds that because everyone has fun through the quixotic exchanges. Sehbai's throwing of a lifeline to him is also in that spirit; of course, with the tacit assurance that the scholarly Mamluk-ul Ali won't take it to heart.

you need to read. Then you will know what metres are used for composing a rubai.'[153]

And so, in this manner an hour or so passed, filled with good-humoured fun, sometimes bordering on the absurd. The audience laughed so hard that tears were flowing from their eyes, and those tears cleared their eyes of any sleep that lingered. It was as if the second part of the mushaira was now getting started and people had only just arrived. Everyone looked fresh after this lively interlude. When people had tired of raising all the various objections and Meer saheb was exhausted from fielding each one with passionate conviction, he announced, 'Hazraat! The ghazal is over!'

The audience responded, 'But, Meer saheb, the maqta has not come yet. How can a ghazal end without the maqta?'

Meer saheb replied, 'The maqta is needed by a poet who wants to tell his audience that this is *his* ghazal.[154] I have no need for a maqta. My ghazal is distinguishable by this unique feature—the moment it begins, everyone knows this can only be Meer saheb's creation and nobody else's!' As he gave this

---

[153]Meer saheb is profoundly mistaken in the subject matter of both the works he mentions, *Mutawwal* and *Arba'een*. It appears that he takes a cue from the sound of words and matches it with books whose names he has heard. Thus, bahr-e-taviil is assumed to be the theme of *Mutawwal*, and rubai is assumed to be discussed in *Arba'een*.

In reality, *Mutawwal* refers to *al-Mutawwal*, a fourteenth-century work on rhetoric, written by Allamah Taftazania, a Persian scholar and master of many sciences. It has nothing at all to do with poetry and metres of ghazal.

Similarly, *Arba'een* refers to Al-Ghazali's *Arba'een Fi Usul ad-Din* (*Forty Principles of the Religion*), a work on religion, and again, having no connection with poetry. Al-Ghazali lived in the eleventh-twelfth century, and is regarded as one of the most influential scholars in Islamic philosophy, jurisprudence and logic. Some of his works, like *Tahafut al-Falasifa* (*Incoherence of Philosophers*) and *Ihya ulum ad-Din* (*Revival of the Religious Sciences*) are read by scholars to this day.

[154]Since the maqta contains the takhallus or pen name of the poet, it links the creator with his creation.

parting shot, he folded his bag and returned to his seat among his friends and well-wishers.

Soon after, one of the lamps was placed before the poet sitting opposite Meer saheb, Mirza Jama'it Shah Maaher. He is the grandson of Badshah Shah Alam Ghazi, the victorious (may his tomb be filled with light), and a pupil of the poet Sabir. His writing is crisp and his language, rich and sweet. He writes:

hum bhi zaruur Kaa'be ko chalte par ab to sheikh
qismat se but-kade hi meiN diidaar ho gaya

naaseh ki baat sunane ka kisko yahaaN dimaaG
tera hi zikr tha ke maiN naachaar ho gaya

ai hum-nashiiN! voh hazrat-e Maaher na hoN kahiiN
ek paarsaa sunaa hai ke mai-KHaar ho gaya

I would surely come to the Holy Kaa'ba, O Sheikh, but now
My good fortune that I found my beloved in the temple itself

Who has the good sense here to listen to good advice
At the mere mention of your name I became helpless

Dear friend! I hope it is not that gentleman Maaher
I heard a virtuous man has become a wine drinker.

Meer saheb's session had rejuvenated everyone despite the late-night hour. As the first ghazal after that, this one got all the praise it deserved and miyaan Maaher tasted the sweet result of his hard work.

After this, the lamp went to Qazi Najamuddin Barq. He belongs to Secunderabad and is about twenty or twenty-two years old. He is tall, has long hair and a wheatish complexion with a faint golden tinge. Overall, he is good looking. He is also good-natured and pleasant with a polite manner of speech and a sunny sense of humour that betrays his easy and carefree attitude to life. He also enjoys his wine. He is wearing a white broad-bottomed loose pyjama like a garara,[155] a white angrakha and a do-palrhi topi. He used to be Momin Khan's shagird, but later, on Momin Khan's advice, he began to obtain corrections from miyaan Taskeen. His voice and style of recitation are attractive and memorable. The ghazal he recited was also praiseworthy. He writes:

bazm-e-aGyaar hai, Dar hai na KHafaa tu ho jaaye
varna ik aah maiN kheNchuN to abhi hu ho jaaye

haram-o-dair ke jhagDe tire chhupne se paDe
varna tu pardaa uTHa de to tu hi tu ho jaaye

kuchh mazaa hai yeh tire ruuTH ke man jaane ka
chaahta huuN yuN hii har roz KHafaa tu ho jaaye

tu to jis KHaak ko chaahe voh bane bandaa-e-paak
maiN Khuda kisko banaa'un jo KHafaa tu ho jaaye

aap inkaar kareN vasl se maiN dar-guzra
kuchh to ho jisse tabiyat miri yaksu ho jaaye

ho na ho bas meiN koi kuchh nahiiN iski parvaah
dil-e-betaab pe, ai Barq! jo qaabu ho jaaye

In this gathering of rivals I'm afraid of offending you
Else I could end the world with a single lovelorn sigh

You remain concealed and so the rift between mosque and temple
If you lift your veil, there would be only you and you

[155]Garara is a loose-fitting women's pyjama, pleated from the knees to fall in waves around the ankles. Here, it implies a pyjama that is more loosely fitted than the usual men's pyjama.

It's charming, your sulking then coming round again
I wish you would sulk this way every day

When you bestow favour on a clay figure it becomes a blessed being
Who should I make my God if you turn away from me

You don't want to meet me, I will forget about it
But there should be some way for me to have a tranquil spirit

Whom I can control and whom I cannot, I don't care
When I can gain control, O Barq, over my wayward heart.

Allah! Allah! An otherworldly rapture overtook the gathering and even the lifeless doors and walls seemed to be caught up in the charm. When the line 'Who should I make my God if you turn away from me' was recited, listeners were hypnotised, what magic it wrought. The ustads were in a state of elation. They repeated the sher themselves, requested for it to be read again and again, and let the stream of the poet's imagination flow deep within their veins.

The spell of his ghazal and the torrent of compliments had not yet fully subsided when the lamp reached to light up Mirza Manjhale who writes with the pen name ' 'Fusuun'. This young man is late Mirza Karim Bakhsh's son, and the grandson of Hazrat Zille Subhani. What can one say of him! He uses the language with consummate ease, as if it were his handmaiden. He does not recite his ghazal, he sings it, and wins people's hearts. I present two shers from his ghazal.

Allah re! Jazba-e dil-e muztar ke tiir ka
baahar hamare pehlu ke sofaar bhi nahiiN

kuchh aap hi aap dil yeh mera baiTHa jaaye hai
zahir meiN to ilahi maiN biimar bhi nahiiN

Allah re! What agony for my impassioned heart that the arrow
Has pierced my side so deep, even its end is not visible

On its own, this heart of mine sinks within
Outwardly there is no ailment, Ilahi, that assails me.

Each word of the second couplet is like a gem, chiselled and fitted with perfection. And why not indeed, his lineage guides him.

After him, the right-hand lamp slid to the side of Lala Balmukund Huzoor. He is about seventy or eighty years of age, a Khatri[156] by caste and a shagird of Khwaja Mir Dard. Even at his age, he has a radiant glow on his face. On top of it, he was dressed in white, with a white Kashmiri scarf on his shoulders. I wanted to keep gazing at him! When the lamp reached him, he pleaded that he was no longer capable of reading, he could only listen to ghazals in the mushaira. But on everyone's insistence, he read this qata:

na paaoN meiN jumbish hai, na haathoN meiN taaqat
jo uTH kheNcheN daaman hum us dilrubaa ka

sare-raah baiTHe haiN aur yeh sadaa hai
ke Allah vali hai be-dast-o-paa ka

I have no vitality in my legs, nor strength in my hands
That I can rise and tug at the hem of the beloved's dress

I'm sitting by the wayside with this prayer on my lips
God is the keeper of the weak limbed and helpless.

He read the qata in a way that he became its very picture. As he recited 'I have no vitality in my legs,' he got up, but his legs gave

[156] The Khatri caste, originating from the Punjab region, dominated in mercantile professions like trading and financial activities. Khatris from Punjab were also scribes during the Mughal period.

way beneath him and he stumbled and sat down again. When he said '...nor strength in my hands,' he raised his hands upward, but enfeebled, they limply fell back to his side. The second line was read faster. On the third line, he adopted the posture of a frail weak-limbed person seated by the wayside, supplicating to the Almighty. And then, he raised his eyes heavenward, once, and read the fourth line, 'God is the keeper of the weak limbed and helpless.'

His performance of the qata infused in the whole mehfil a wondrous spirit of humble realisation and instead of the typical compliments, everyone spontaneously repeated the last line, 'God is the keeper of the weak limbed and helpless.'

Ustad Zauq was deeply moved. He said, 'This is a divine gift and the grace of Khwaja Mir Dard. Subhan-allah! What an inspirational kalaam. Only a teacher like Mir Dard can produce this kind of inspired effect on worldly ones like us.'

After this, who would have paid heed to the ghazal of Mirza Ghulam Muhiuddin Ashki? He is the grandson of Badshah Shah Alam Ghazi. He is about forty years old. Tall in stature, with a grave expression, he is attired all in white. He used to obtain corrections from Nizamuddin Mamnuun earlier, now he is Mufti Sadruddin's shagird. He had written:

kuchh vajd nahiiN naGma-e-mutrib hi pe mauquuf
kaafi hai yahaaN naalaa-e-berabt diraa ka

sajde meiN gire dekh ke tasviir-e-but Ashki
maaluum hua aapka KHirqa tha riya ka

My ecstasy does not only arise from a singer's melody
Enough is the discordant lament of the caravan bell

Ashki fell in sajda when he saw the beloved's image
Later realised that the patched robe was but a pretence.

After him, the lamp went to Sahebzade Abbas Ali Khan Betaab. He must be about thirty or thirty-two years old. He is from Rampur and is Momin Khan's shagird. He is friendly with Nawab Mustafa Khan Shefta and has accompanied him to the mushaira. He read his ghazal in a high tone, as if he were reading a prose piece. The ghazal itself was not exceptional, but on the other hand, the qata, in which he described the tavern with its minutiae, certainly deserved praise. Subhan-allah! Here is what he recited:

maa'mur hai Khuda ki inaayat se maikadaa
saqi agar nahiiN hai, na ho, mai se kaam hai

betaab pii, Khuda ne tujhe bhi diye haiN haath
yeh KHum hai, yeh sabu hai, yeh shiishaa, yeh jaam hai

The tavern is flourishing by the grace of God
If the saqi is missing, never mind, wine is your concern

Betaab, help yourself, God has given you hands
Here the wine barrel, the pitcher, here the flask and wine cup.

Now the lamp came to Mirza Fakhruddin Hashmat. Was it really necessary for him to read at such a big mushaira? Neither was his kalaam any good, nor his recitation and cadence. But then who could stop him? He is a prince, and that too, Badshah Shah Alam's grandson. Anyway, he read his ghazal and his relatives and friends praised it too. He looked pleased. This was his ghazal:

tire biimar-e hijraaN ka tire bin
yeh aalam hai ke aalam nauhaagar hai

mujhe rote jo dekha haNs ke bole
mire Hashmat! bataa kyuN chashm tar hai

The state of your lovesick suitor without you
Is as if the entire state is a mourner that laments

When she saw me weeping, she asked with a laugh
My Hashmat! Tell me, why are your eyes wet?

After him, the lamp came to someone who is a poet even at this young age, and will be a poet of repute in all of Hindustan. Tell me, which is that mushaira in which the ghazal of Mirza Qurbaan Ali Beg Salik is not heard with the greatest delight, and which is that sher that is not asked to be read again and again? If you have gone to a mushaira even once, you will know him from afar. He is short and has slender hands and legs; a large nose, beady eyes, a wheatish skin with pockmarks on his face. His beard is scanty on his cheeks, but fills out on his chin. His hair is short and thin. He is about thirty years old and can be mistaken for a Turk from Bukhara. Of course, his attire is very different from theirs. He wore a low-bodiced angrakha and a narrow-bottomed pyjama along with a white round cap on his head and a white handkerchief in his hand. When the lamp reached him, the audience sat up attentively. He too prepared himself: rolled up the sleeves of his angrakha and straightened his cap. Then he threw a glance towards his ustad Mirza Ghalib. There came some unspoken signal from Ghalib, and Salik turned to Saheb-e-alam and said, 'Do I have your leave?'

Mirza Fakhru replied, 'Go ahead, miyaan Salik, recite your ghazal. My permission is not needed!'

Salik took out a piece of paper from his pocket, turned it this way and that, then sat up and read this ghazal:

intahaa sabr aazmaai ki
hai daraazi shab-e-judaai ki

hai buraai nasiib ki ke mujhe
tumse ummiid hai bhalaai ki

naqsh hai sang-e-aastaaN pe tere
daastaaN apni jabha-saai ki

hai fuGaaN baad-e-imtihaan-e-fuGaaN
phir shikaayat hai na-rasaai ki

kya na karta visaal shaadi-e marg
tumne kyuN mujh se bevafaai ki

raaz khulte gaye mire sab par
jis qadr usne KHudnumaai ki

kitne aajiz haiN hum ke paate haiN
bande-bande meiN buu KHudaai ki

rah gayiN dil meiN hasrateN Salik
aa gayi umr paarsaai ki

My patience is being tested to the greatest limit
The night of separation stretches too long

The fault is in my stars that I nurse
The hope for your kindness

On the stones of your threshold is etched
The long story of my adoration

I'm lamenting that even after all my pitiful laments
Not being sincere is your complaint of me

This union led to my death by happiness
Why were you unfaithful to me?

My heart's secrets were exposed slowly
As her vanity increased

How forlorn in the world I am, I find
The breath of God in every person

My heart remains full of old longings, Salik
And already the age of piety is upon me.

Every couplet elicited an ecstatic response, every couplet was made to be repeated over and over, every word got praise and every metaphor met with exuberant appreciation.

On the third sher, Ustad Zauq commented, 'Wah, miyaan Salik, I don't have the words to praise this! Many poets have woven the word "jabha-saai", "adoration" in their couplets, but none has told the daastaan quite like you. What expression, and how smoothly and seamlessly it flows. Subhan-allah!'

Hakim Momin Khan said, 'Miyaan Salik, in this youth, why this theme of old age in your maqta? There's still a long time to go before your "umr-e-paarsaai", your "age of piety". Right now, you must not speak of old age and be like old people!'

Salik replied, 'Ustad, I have grown old in my youth. Who knows if I'm destined to see old age at all?[157] And then, why ignore a mazmuun that troubles the heart? After all, nobody will be concerned afterwards about whether the sher had been written by a young fellow or an old man. We will not remain forever, but the mazmuun will live on.'

When the comments and waves of wah-wahs ebbed away, the lamp passed to Mirza Rahimuddin Ijad. He is the son of Shehzada Mirza Husain Bakhsh and the pupil of Maulana Sehbai. He is about twenty-four or twenty-five years old. He writes poetry, but it is somewhat colourless. Yes, his style of recitation is very good and he sings well. His mellifluous singing is, in fact, able to cover up the weaknesses in his composition.

but-KHane meiN tha ya ke Kaa'be ke qariiN tha
ai zahid-e naadaaN! tujhe kya, maiN kahiiN tha

[157]Qurbaan Ali Beg Salik was born in Hyderabad and brought up in Delhi. After the 1857 Uprising, he moved to Alwar and was later associated with the education department of the government of Hyderabad. He died in 1880, at the age of about sixty.

har chand ke maiN dost ke hamraah nahiiN tha
par dil voh balaa hai voh jahaaN tha, yeh vahiiN tha

toDa hai yeh kuchh aap ko maine, ke jahaaN meiN
saabit na raha naam ka jo mere nagiiN tha

I was in the temple or near the Kaa'ba
O innocent devotee! What is it to you where I was

Every moment when I was not present with my friend
My wayward heart nonetheless was where she was

I have crushed my self such that in the world
The gem that was my name is no longer intact.

The ghazal itself was ordinary, but his singing was especially pleasing. Singing of the verses is an innovation, a new colour that started with the princes of the Qila. The ustads, however, do not commend this style.

Now the lamp came to Nawab Alauddin Khan Alai. He read his ghazal in a powerful and ringing voice. He is one of Mirza Ghalib's much-loved shagirds. He is still young, but already his verses have polish. And why not, whose pupil is he after all? Read his ghazal, it mirrors his ustad Ghalib's style.[158]

aavaargaan-e gulkadah aazo aarzuu!
haasha gar tumheN sar-e-siir-o-faraaG hai

rakhiyo sambhal ke paaoN, jo biina ho chashm-e-dil
kiijo samajh ke kaam, jo roshan dimaaG hai

voh gul jo aaj hai qadah-e-mauj KHez-e-rang
voh lal jo ke baaG ka chashm-o-charaaG hai

[158]Mirza Ghalib was known for his cerebral style. He drew upon uncommon or new themes and a lot of his work is metaphysical in nature, with layers of interpretations.

gul chuur kal hai sang-e-jafaa-e-shahr se
goya ke Gam-kade ka shikasta ayaaG hai

aur laal tund baad-e-havaadis se KHaak-o-KHuN
goya dil-o-jigar ka kisike voh daaG hai

jis jaa ke thaa tarana-e-bulbul nashaat KHez
us jaa pe aaj dil shikan aavaaz-e zaaG hai

maGruur-e jah se yeh kaho tum Alaiya!
kal ek sub.h-e KHaak hai, jo aaj baaG hai

O wanderers, searching for bedecked gardens
Beware, if you desire leisure in fresh air

Step carefully, seeing with the eyes of your heart
Act wisely with your enlightened mind

The rose that is the cup of gaiety, the hue of ecstasy
The tulip that is the light of the garden today

Tomorrow that rose will be crushed by the cruel city
Like a broken cup of woe lying vanquished

And that tulip will be gore and ash left behind by violent calamities
Like a scar on somebody's wounded heart

Where once the bulbul's melody echoed with exuberant joy
There the crow's cacophony wrinkles the heart today

Tell the imperious and arrogant, O Alaiya!
Tomorrow will be arid dust, what is a garden today.

From Alai the lamp moved to Mirza Karimuddin Rasa who sat up alert in anticipation. Thereafter, he read a long ghazal, but all of it was ineffective; neither the words were well woven, nor the theme meaningful. I was irked by the knotted phrases, and the word soup hurt my sensibility. I will present only two couplets here to give you a taste of his ghazal... that will be enough!

baaz aa, sataa tu mujh ko bohat ishva-gar nahiiN
karta kisi pe zulm koi is qadar nahiiN

go naza'a meiN huuN maiN tire bin, aae jaan-e-man!
karne kii jaan bhi mire tan se safar nahiiN

Please refrain, don't trouble me so much
Nobody tyrannises someone like this

Even if without you I'm on my last breath, my love
Life will not journey from my body like this.

After him, it was the turn of Nawab Ziauddin Khan Nayyar Rakhshaan. He writes very well in Persian, but in Urdu, his poetry is dull. He writes:

piike girne ka hai khayaal hameN
saqiya, lijiyo sambhaal hameN

shab na aaye jo apne vaade par
guzre kya-kya na ehtemaal hameN

dil meiN mazhar haiN maa'ni baqii
kisii surat nahiiN zavaal hameN

tere Gusse ne ek dam meiN kiya
murda nuh hazaar saal hameN

taala-e-bad se Nayyar-e Rakhshaan
apne hi ghar meiN hai vabaal hameN

I want to falter after drinking
O saqi, lend me a helping hand

She did not come last night as she promised
What doubts and fears assailed my heart

Purpose and intent remain pulsing through my heart
I'm not ready in the least for my decline

Your anger turned me in one moment
Into a corpse of nine thousand years

It's great misfortune, Nayyar Rakhshaan
To experience such ruin and wreck in my own house.

After him, the lamp went to the side of Mirza Pyare Rafat. He is about forty years of age and is a salatin living in the Qila. He is very fond of quail fighting. He also writes good poetry. Initially, he was a pupil of Ehsaan; now he is in the discipleship of Maulana Sehbai. He writes:

basaan-e-tair-e-rang-e-pareeda vahshat se
kise dimaaG hai ab aashiyaaN banaane ka

na uzr tha hameN hone meiN KHaak ke, gar hum
yeh jaante ke voh daaman nahiiN bachaane ka

gundhhi thii kaun se badmast-e-tishna lab ki voh KHaak
ke jis se KHum yeh banaa hai sharaab-KHaane ka

ba-zauq naaz ko de ruKHsat-e-jafaa ke yahaaN
hameN bhi azm hai taaqat ke aazmaane ka

haiN ik voh bhi ke tumse hai jin ko raaz-o-niyaaz
aur ik hum haiN ke takte haiN muNh zamaane ka

Beware of the madness of birds of fading colours
Who has the courage now to build a nest

I would not hesitate to humble myself into a grain of dust
If I had known she would not stay aloof, apart

What heady thirst of the lips was kneaded in the clay
With which the wine cup in the tavern is made

Bid farewell to your cold-hearted vanity and coquetry
For I am also bent on testing my strength against my rivals

There are those that have gained your confidence and favour
And here am I, staring emptily at the world from afar.

The last sher paints a melancholy image that is indescribable. There was nobody there who remained untouched by the mood it created, and who did not repeat the second line to savour, all the deeper, its anguish. There was nobody who did not acknowledge its simple elegance with a wah-wah or Subhan-allah.

And so, by and by, many poets read their ghazals until finally, it was miyaan Arif's turn. I wondered when he had found the time to write a ghazal for the mushaira, considering how much time he'd spent in organising it. It seemed, however, that he had managed to pen something even though he had been completely preoccupied day and night. I was amazed at what he had written, it was quite remarkable.

uTHta qadam jo aage ko, ai naamaah-bar nahiiN
peechhe to chhoD aaye kahiiN uska ghar nahiiN

auroN ko ho to ho, hameN marne se Dar nahiiN
KHat leke hum hi jaate haiN gar naamaah-bar nahiiN

be-iltefatiyoN ka tiri shikva kya kareN
apne hi jab ke naalaa-e-dil meiN asar nahiiN

That your feet refuse to proceed another step, O postman
Is it possible you have left her house somewhere behind?

Others may be afraid of death and dying, I have no fear
I will carry the letter myself if the messenger does not

What should I complain of your coldness towards me
When the lamenting of my heart has no effect on you.

Everyone praised the opening couplet. Ustad Ehsaan said, 'Miyaan Arif! I have grown old writing ghazals. I have heard millions of shers, and millions I have recited. But this theme is completely new and how deftly you have laid it out—truly pleasing to my heart!'

After Arif, the lamp came to Mirza Ghulam Nasiruddin alias Mirza Manjhale. He is a prince and a shagird of Ehsaan. He writes under the pen name 'Qana'at' and he writes exceptional ghazals. In fact, I will go on to say that among the princes, there would be very few fine poets like him. His ghazal went like this:

shauq ko kasrat-e-nazaaraa se rashk aata hai
hashr se pehle mayyassar ho voh diidaar mujhe

Kaa'be tak jaane meiN thi KHatir-e-zahid, varna
dair meiN bhi thi sadaa ruKHsat-e-diidaar mujhe

jins-e duzdiida ki maanind hai uljhaao meiN jaan
ke na leta hai na phere hai KHariidaar mujhe

raaz-e-dil lab pe na laana kabhi Mansur ke yaN
kar diya baat ke kehne ne gunahgaar mujhe

My desire is envious of the abundance of vision
If only I can catch a glimpse of it before the Day of Judgement

I went to the Kaa'ba out of respect for the pious one
Otherwise, I could always behold my beloved in the temple

Like stolen goods my life is in confusion
The buyer does not take me nor give me back to my owner

Don't ever bring your heart's secret to your lips like Mansur[159]
Uttering my heart's secret aloud only made me a sinner.

The lamp now moved to Hakim Aaga Jaan Aish and excited a lot of murmurs and whispers in the gathering. Hakim saheb comes from a family of royal physicians. Embellished with the jewel of knowledge and adorned with fine clothes, he is a cultured man. Sunny natured, sweet tongued and always cheerful, whenever one sees him, he seems to be smiling. He is witty and has a flair for humour. Subhan-allah! Physically, Hakim Aaga Jaan is trim and of medium height, with one inch of his hair-roots on the head showing grey. His beard follows the same trend. And with his fair ruddy complexion, these come together to make for a pleasing effect. His crinkled and crisp white muslin kurta resembles a heap of jasmine flowers encircling his neck.

But for some days now, he has drifted away from his friends. By cultivating miyaan Hudhud, he has hurt his relationship with everyone else. In the beginning, nobody paid much attention to Hudhud's crazy and hurtful comments. But when he began to overreach and take aim at the ustads, then along with Hudhud, Hakim Aaga Jaan also lost everyone's affection. The worst outrage came when Hakim saheb himself launched a frontal attack on Mirza Nausha at the Ajmeri Gate mushaira by reciting this qata.

agar apna kahaa tum aap hi samjhe to kya samjhe
mazaa kehne ka jab hai, ik kahe aur duusra samjhe

kalaam-e-Mir samjhe aur zabaan-e-Mirza samjhe
magar inka kahaa, ya aap samjheN ya Khuda samjhe

If you alone grasp what you write then what good is it
The delight in writing is, one writes and the other follows

[159]This is again a reference to Mansur al-Hallaj, Sufi mystic and teacher.

The words of Mir were well understood as also the
language of Mirza[160]
But what he writes only he understands or his God.

Maulvi Mamluk-ul Ali remonstrated, 'Hakim saheb, not understanding a sher can only be attributed to two things: either the sher lacks substance or the listener's mind lacks the power to grasp its meaning. We all understand his poetry well enough; why do you count us poor folks with yourself?'[161]

Momin Khan said, 'Bhai, in the third line of this qata, I detect the poet's own vanity and pompousness!'

Anyway, the affair was ultimately resolved with great difficulty.

After that fateful mushaira, this was the second time Hakim Aaga Jaan was present at a mushaira. Earlier in the evening, he had heard, with some trepidation, Meer saheb's proclamation of war on Hudhud with his hajv. Now he saw everyone muttering and whispering among themselves, and he became still more perturbed. He hesitated to read, but finally, when Mirza Fakhru urged him, he recited this ghazal:

sulah unse hameN kiye hi banii
dil pe jhagDa tha, dil diye hi banii

zuhd-o-taqva dhare rahe saare
haath se uske mai piye hi banii

---

[160]'Mir' refers to Mir Taqi Mir and 'Mirza' is Mirza Muhammad Rafi Sauda.

[161]Ghalib was often criticised for writing dense verses that could not be easily grasped by one and all. On one occasion, Maulvi Abdul Qadir of Rampur told Ghalib that he couldn't understand one verse of his, then went ahead and recited this made-up verse, 'First take the essence of the rose / out of the eggs of buffaloes / and other drugs are there, take those / out of the eggs of buffaloes.' Ghalib was taken aback and said he had not written it. But Abdul Qadir insisted he had read it in Ghalib's divan. At length, Ghalib understood the criticism being levelled at him and his poetry. Of course, his characteristic response to such fault-finding was to be dismissive. Pavan K. Varma, *Ghalib: The Man, the Times*, 2008, pp. 126–27.

laaye voh saath Gair ko naachaar
paas apne baiTHa liye hi banii

kiska thaa paas-e-shauq-e-zulm, ai Aish!
in jafaaoN pe bhi jiye hi banii

I made up with him after the disagreement, it had to be
A dispute of hearts it was, I gave up mine, it had to be

Religion and piety were gently set aside
When he offered me wine, I had not the heart to deny

He brought my rival along with him
I could not help seating him beside me

O Aish, who can claim to revel in pain and suffering
In spite of all injustices, life had to be lived.

When a ghazal is at such a level of fullness and is so apt, who can help but appreciate it? Voices calling out Salle-'alaa and Subhan-allah resounded through the mehfil, washing over the poet and the listeners, and all hearts were cleansed of ill-feeling and antagonism. Hakim saheb became the old Hakim saheb and no longer did anyone bear him any grudge; in turn, he too shook off his own regret and brooding. All this, thanks to the alchemy of his ghazal!

Of course, who knows what the hue of the mushaira might have been if miyaan Hudhud had gained sway earlier in the evening. May God keep him safe, our good Meer saheb, that he silenced that strange bird right at the very start and averted any further misadventure.

After Hakim saheb, next in line was Mirza Rahimuddin Haya. He is the same miyaan Haya who had been sarcastically glorified, in absentia, by his father Mirza Karimuddin Rasa upon the latter's arrival at the mushaira. Mirza Haya is about thirty-five or thirty-six years old and lives mostly in Benaras, visiting Dehli off and on. He is a genial, intelligent and kind-hearted person with an easy sense of humour. He looks exactly like a prince, but he is clean-shaven and dresses up in the Lucknawi style. He started out being his father's pupil, then he obtained corrections for his work from Shah Nasir and now he takes his poetry to Ustad Zauq for revision. He is an excellent chess player too. He learnt chess from Hakim Ashraf Ali Khan, but now he goes to Hakim Momin Khan to discuss his chess problems. If this is not all, he has proficiency in playing the sitar as well. He is a good poet, but he doesn't put in too much work into his poetry. He sacrifices meaning for the frills of language. This is the ghazal he had brought:

maut hi chaara-saaz-e-furqat hai
ranj marne ka, mujh ko raahat hai

ho chuka vasl, vaqt-e-ruKHsat hai
ai ajal jald aa ke fursat hai

roz ki daad kaun devega
zulm karna tumhari aadat hai

kaarvaan umr ka hai raKHt badosh
har nafs baang-e-kos-e-rehlat hai

saans ek phaaNs-si khaTakti hai
dam nikalta nahiiN musiibat hai

tum bhi apne Haya ko dekh aao
aaj uski kuchh aur haalat hai

Death is the only remedy for the pain of staying apart
There's no sorrow in death, only relief and ease of heart

The hour of union is past, it is now time to part
O death! Hurry, for now I have the leisure to depart

Who will praise you day after day
To inflict pain and suffering is your habit

The procession of life weighs heavy on my shoulders
Every breath is an awakening call of the caravan bell

My breath is stuck like a thorn lodged in my throat
Life does not ebb away, it's a painful bother

Come, see how your Haya fares
Today his state is beyond repair.

On the fifth sher, 'My breath is stuck like a thorn in my throat / Life does not ebb away, it's a painful bother', his father stopped him and said, 'Miyaan Haya, you changed your physical appearance when you went to Lucknow…now you have changed your style of language too. I see you used the word "saans" in the feminine gender.'

Haya answered, 'No sir! I have followed Ustad Zauq's example. He writes: "The breath will constrict the chest in some time…"'[162]

But Saheb-e-alam Mirza Rasa would not be so easily convinced. He retorted, 'Can your ustad's kalaam be a certificate against my word? He can write whatever he wishes. Tell me, in the convention used in the Qila, is the word "saans" used in the masculine or feminine gender?'[163]

Poor Haya, he just smiled and fell silent.

Now the lamp came before Maulana Sehbai. He is well-known all over Hindustan for his intellect and knowledge. Such an extraordinarily accomplished person is rare. He has thousands of pupils who write rekhta, and he gives them guidance and

---

[162]Ustad Zauq's line that Haya cites uses the word 'saans' in the feminine gender, in much the same way as Haya has originally used it in his own ghazal.

[163]This exchange is a typical example of the variations in Urdu as it was spoken in Delhi and Awadh. Delhi was regarded as the nucleus of Urdu given its long cultural tradition of the development of the tongue, as well as due to the Mughal patronage Urdu received. It was natural, therefore, for Delhi poets and members of the royalty to be somewhat snobbish and intolerant of the Lucknawi stylistic elements in the tongue.

revisions—excellent guidance and perfectly apt revisions. But his own work, all of it superlative, is in Persian. I have never heard or read his ghazal in rekhta. In this mushaira too, he recited a ghazal in Persian. He received a lot of accolades of course, but to tell the truth, people did not genuinely enjoy it.

hum chu shabnam KHesh ra fariG za aalam saaKHtam
mahram-e-KHurshiid gashtam, ba-KHasaN kam saaKHtam

murdam va dar chashm-e-mardam aalam-e-taariik gasht
man magar shama'am, chu raftam, bazm barham saaKHtam

kufr dar kesham sipaas-e-nemat-e-diidaar ust
jalva-dar har rang diidam gardan-e-KHam saaKHtam

jurm-e-ishqam ra jaza shad ho ruu man az mehr-e-dost
daaG bar-dil bardam va KHuldash jahannam saaKHtam

niist Sehbai jo jaam-e-jam nasiibam go mabaad
mai za KHuun-e-dil kashiidam KHesh ra jam saaKHtam

My form is embellished like a dew drop
My close companion is the sun most noble

When I died the whole world grew dark
Was I the light that slowly disarrayed the mehfil?

It is heresy to be grateful for a sight of my beloved
When I can bow my head and behold her form in everything

The crime of love is praiseworthy, my face mirrors the sun
With the mark on my heart, hell turns into paradise

O Sehbai, if you are destined not to possess the cup of Jamshid[164]

[164]In Persian mythology, the cup of Jamshid was possessed by the rulers of Iran.

I'll make a bowl of my self and wine from the blood of my heart.

On the last sher, the encomiums he got surpass all description. But there were those who did not understand Persian and they remained clueless and unimpressed. To be clear, the foisting of a Persian ghazal upon an Urdu mushaira did not really appeal to me.

But moving on…ahhha! If you want to luxuriate in the delights of the tongue, then listen to Syed Zahiruddin Khan Zahir. He is about thirty or thirty-two years of age, and by the grace of the Almighty, his poetry speaks to you. Wah-wah! And Ustad Zauq's islah is the icing on the cake!

Zahir's appearance is deceptive and just by looking at him, it is impossible to know of his poetically sensitive temperament. He has a spare build, is broad-chested and dusky-complexioned with a long straight nose, bright eyes that are neither too large nor too small, and a well-defined jawline. Sporting a round-cut beard neither too full nor too sparse and shoulder-length hair, he makes for a striking figure. He was dressed in an angrakha, a narrow-bottomed pyjama and a round white cap on his head. He is pleasant with an easy light-hearted demeanour and is soft spoken. His style of reading resembles the Lucknow taht ul-lafz style.[165] Side by side, he also uses hand gestures to explain the words in his ghazal, and that makes it come alive. This was his ghazal.

jabiN aur shauq uske aastaaN ka
iraada aur iraada bhi kahaaN ka

It was discovered in Persepolis in ancient times and was said to be filled with the elixir of immortality. All seven heavens could be observed in it and divinations from it could reveal profound truths.

[165]In this style, the ghazal or other poetic piece is not sung, but spoken, with each word and syllable clearly enunciated.

luTa hai qafila taab-e-tavaaN ka
Khuda hafiz hai dil ke kaarvaaN ka

miri vaamaandgi manzil rasaaN hai
suraaG-e-naqsh-e pa hoN kaarvaaN ka

rahe paaband dil ke dil meiN armaaN
qadam manzil ne pakDa kaarvaaN ka

uTHa sakte nahiiN sar aastaaN se
ghazab hai baar-e-minnat paasbaaN ka

hamesha morid-e-barq-o-balaa hoN
miTe jhagDa ilahi aashiyaaN ka

dil-e-betaab ne voh bhi miTaya
kisii ko kuchh jo dhoka tha fuGaaN ka

Zahir! aao chalo ab mai-kade ko
nikaala zuhd-o-taqvaa hai kahaaN ka

I yearn to bow my head at the threshold of the beloved
The intention, and that too for what place!

Processions of the strong and powerful have been ruined
Only God can protect the caravan of the heart

I have fallen behind and my destination beckons
Let my footprints give a clue of the caravan on its way

My heart's wishes remained encased within my heart
The destination fell in step with my voyage on its part

I cannot lift my head from the threshold of the beloved
My prayer to the protector overwhelms me with its weight

I am always the target of calamities
If only there were no nest at all, Ilahi, to smite

The restless heart's turmoil has also dispelled
The false notion of loud lamenting in sorrow deeply felt

Zahir! Come, let's go now to the tavern
What good is all this piety and abstinence?

What's more, the masters showered so much praise for this ghazal that miyaan Zahir was gratified like a newly flowered bud. On the third couplet, 'I have fallen behind and my destination beckons / Let my footprints give a clue of the caravan on its way', there was unending applause from so many people that I'm sure Zahir's hands were exhausted from acknowledging each of them with gracious salaams.

Finally when silence prevailed, the right side lamp came in front of Nawab Mustafa Khan Shefta. What does one say of him? He is counted among the masters of verse. He is Momin Khan's shagird, but he himself has many pupils. If a sher receives his seal of approval by way of praise, it gains respect and memorability among poetry lovers. If, on the other hand, a sher encounters silence, its weight and worth take a nosedive. Nawab Shefta is one who places great emphasis on mazmuun, while also paying loving attention to the tongue and usage of words and phrases. When he reads a ghazal in his sonorous voice, he goes to the trouble of explaining each word. The effect is that everyone seated anywhere in the room can hear him clearly and everyone partakes in his ghazal recitation actively.[166]

Before he began reciting, he looked this way and that, adjusted his cap and angrakha, rolled up the ends of the sleeves and

[166]Presentation of one's work in public was an art and a craft that was of paramount significance in a time when there was no technology to aid the poets' recitation and reach—their tone and style of delivery was all they had. Every poet, therefore, developed their own signature style and that became inseparable from their poetry. Use of hand gestures, or singing the ghazal (in whole or part), or reciting in a particular cadence, even the rare 'performance' of the ghazal were all part of a poet's toolkit.

then he read this ghazal:

aaram se hai kaun jahaan-e-KHaraab meiN
gul siina chaak aur sabaa iztiraab meiN

sab is meiN mahav aur yeh sab se alaheda
aaine meiN hai aab, na aaina aab meiN

ma'ni ki fikr chahiye, surat se kya husuul
kya faaeda hai mauj agar hai saraab meiN

zaat-o-sifaat meiN bhi yehi rabt chahiye
juN aaftaab-o roshni-e-aaftaab meiN

voh qatra huN ke mauja-e-darya meiN gum hua
voh saaya huN ke mahav hua aaftaab meiN

bebaak sheva, shoKH tabiyat, zabaaN daraaz
mulzim hua hai par nahiiN aajiz jawaab meiN

takliif Shefta hui tumko magar huzuur!
is vaqt ittefaq se voh hain 'itaab meiN

Who in this ruined world is at peace
The bosom of the rose is carved, flustered is the gentle breeze

Everyone is immersed in it and the world remains out of reach
The mirror does not shine nor is it in the water

What's to be gained in appearance, true meaning should be sought
What good is the gleam of water if it gleams in a mirage

The person and persona must have the same kinship
As the sun has with the light rays of the sun

I am the drop that is lost in the waves of the river
I am the shadow that diffused in the light of the sun

Fearless in manner, exuberant in spirit, forthright in words
Enchained sinner he may be, but not helpless in the world

You have been put to great trouble, Shefta, but dear sir!
In this moment, incidentally, he is in a state of anger.

The ghazal is profound and packed with sage insights—who could possibly praise it as much as it properly merited? Thus, appreciation was given with due consideration.

In large mushairas, I have found that young budding poets are given great encouragement with enthusiastic words of praise. But when it comes to established poets and masters of verse, then the raw enthusiasm and instant accolades are replaced by maturity and depth of thought. For an ustad, only those couplets are praised that are truly remarkable. If a sher is accorded empty praise just like that, the ustad feels cheated. After all, he knows which of his shers are outstanding and he expects only those to be acknowledged by other masters. So too, while reading the ghazal, the ustad's eyes travel to his equals to seek their opinion and those peers, in turn, give their authentic appreciation. The others in the mushaira enjoy the masters' works, while at the same time, learning from them. For ghazals by masters are no less than an islah by them, and of great significance for the same reason.

Then came the turn of Shehzada Mirza Qadir Bakhsh Sabir. He is about forty years old and his work is quite famous in the Qila. Why, he himself is quite proud of his poetry! He is working on a tazkirah of the poets of Dehli, but the grapevine suggests that it is actually the work of Maulana Sehbai, from start to finish. Only God knows whether this is the truth or just an empty rumour. He has penned his thoughts about himself in a qata that I share here.

pehle ustad the Ehsaan-o Nasir-o Momin
hui ehsaN se pur islaah-e-tabiyat meri

phir hua hazrat-e-Sehbai ki islah ka faiz
taba' baariik hui unki badaulat meri

aur hum-bazm rahe Momin-o-Zauq-o-Ghalib
ustaadoN hi se har dam rahi sohbat meri

Hind ka fazl-o-hunar zaat pe hai jin ki tamaam
maante haiN vahi ashKHaas faziilat meri

mun'aqid hoti hai jab shahr meiN bazm-e-inshaad
karte haiN ahl-e-sukhan vaq'at-o izzat meri

At the start my teachers were Ehsaan, Nasir and Momin
I was indebted to them for their guidance

Then I had the grace of hazrat Sehbai's islah
From him I learnt the nuances of poetics

And I found the company of Momin, Ghalib and Zauq
All the time I was with respected ustads

For whom the only creed is knowledge and accomplishment
Such learned people acknowledge my clout

Wherever in the city there's a gathering of learned men
Men of letters regard me with utmost respect.

Now, on the basis of this kalaam, I can regard him as an ustad or not. In the ghazal he read, there's a similar vapidity. Even so, the entire city considers him an ustad. Who knows, maybe he is an ustad, or maybe it's my lack of understanding. Here's the ghazal he recited.

nazaaraa barq-e-husn ka dushvaar ho gaya
jalva hijaab-e-diidah-e bedaar ho gaya

mehfil meiN to us lab-e-mai goN ke saamne
naam-e sharaab leke gunahgaar ho gaya

ha'il hui naqaab to THehrii nigaah-e-shauq
pardaa hi jalva-gaah-e ruKH-e-yaar ho gaya

maaluum yeh hua ke hai pursish gunaah ki
aasi gunaah na karda gunahgaar ho gaya

uski gali meiN aan ke kya-kya uTHaye ranj
KHaak-e-shifaa mili to maiN biimaar ho gaya

piirii meiN humko qata'-e-ta'alluq hua nasiib
qaamat KHamiida hote hi talvaar ho gaya

It was impossible to look upon the beloved's flashing beauty
Her beauty itself became the veil

In the mehfil in front of her wine-lips
The screen itself became her beauty

My desirous eyes stopped as her veil came in the way
The nuptial chamber's screen reflected my beloved's face

I learnt that upon asking questions about sin
The miscreant is a sinner even when he commits no sin

What all trouble I had to take to come to her lane
The curing dust made me sick

In old age I had the fortune to sever the bond
I turned into a sword when my feeble back bent.

After he finished reading, the lamp went to Mufti Sadruddin Aazurda. Scholars of his stature do not often write poetry; when they do, they are counted among masters of verse. So it is with Mufti Aazurda. Several of his pupils are intellectuals; and several more are poets, brilliant poets at that. Mufti saheb writes magnificent poetry and he recites it expertly. His style is that of a teacher delivering a lesson to his attentive pupils in a low and measured tone. His dignified presence is such that the mehfil is cocooned in reverential silence through his reading, and only exceptional shers are applauded, in a suitably low polite tone.

Of course, Mirza Nausha does not desist from joking with him in his typical light-hearted manner, sometimes even contradicting some emotion or thought expressed in a particular sher. And thus, easy banter sprinkles the ghazal recitation with a warmth of spirit. This is his ghazal, see how well-formed and well-articulated his thoughts are.

naaloN se mere kab tah-o-baalaa jahaaN nahiiN
kab aasmaaN zamiin-o zamiiN aasmaaN nahiiN

afsurdah dil na ho dar-e-rahmat nahiiN hai band
kis din khula hua dar-e piir-e-muGaaN nahiiN

shab usko haal-e-dil ne jataayaa kuchh is tarah
haiN lab to kya, nigaah bhi hui tarjumaaN nahiiN

ai dil! tamaam nafaa hai saudaa-e-ishq meiN
ik jaan ka ziyaaN hai so aisa ziyaaN nahiiN

kaTti kisi tarah bhi nahiiN yeh shab-e-firaaq
shaayad ke gardish aaj tujhe aasmaaN nahiiN

kehta huN us se kuchh meiN, nikalta hai muNh se kuchh
kehne ko yuN to haigi zabaaN aur zabaaN nahiiN

Aazurda! honT tak na hile us ke ruu-ba-ruu
maanaa ke aap-sa koi jaadu-bayaaN nahiiN

When has my passionate cry failed to upturn the world
When could it not stand earth on heaven, bring heaven
to earth

Let not your heart feel forlorn, the portals of mercy are not shut
Is there any day the tavern-keeper did not open his door?

So expertly the night impressed upon her the state of my heart
What of lips, even the eyes for words had no regard

Dear heart! The trade in love always starts and ends in profit
The only loss is that of life, and there's nothing to it

This night of separation does not pass, no matter how I try
Maybe the heavens hesitate in their revolution tonight

I mean to say something and my tongue utters something else
My tongue is in name only, it seems good for nothing else

Aazurda! Face to face with her, your lips were unable to even move
And to say, there's nobody to match the magic of your speech.

After Aazurda's reading came Nawab Mirza Khan Daagh. It was an unusual transition—from an authority like Aazurda to Daagh, a young budding poet. There are two things however: First, everyone is fond of Daagh and immensely encouraging of his talent, knowing that someday in the future, this very Daagh will be the light of the cultural realm of Hindustan. Second, the ghazal Daagh presented won the hearts of the masters, and Mirza Fakhru's belief was upheld that this young poet rightfully belonged among the ustads. It was extraordinary for a seventeen- or eighteen-year-old to compose such an awe-inspiring ghazal and to read it with such bold confidence.

It is my opinion that the form and language used by this young poet are genuinely unique and certainly not in everyone's domain of skill and craft. See for yourself, his bejewelled language, the thematic hue and that impressive fluency in metre, and give him abundant praise.

saaz yeh kiina saaz kya jaaneN
naaz vaale niyaaz kya jaaneN

shama ru aap go hue lekin
lutf-o-soz-o-gudaaz kya jaaneN

kab kisi dar ki jabha-sai' kii
sheikh saheb namaaz kya jaaneN

jo raah-e-ishq meiN qadam rakkheN
voh nasheb-o-faraaz kya jaaneN

puchhiye mai-kashoN se lutf-e-sharaab
yeh mazaa pakbaaz kya jaaneN

jin ko apni KHabar nahiiN ab tak
voh mere dil ka raaz kya jaaneN

hazrat-e Khizr jab shahiid na hoN
lutf-e umr-e-daraaz kya jaaneN

jo guzarte haiN Daagh pe sadme
aap banda-navaaz kya jaaneN

What do the small-hearted know of joining hearts?
How can the self-important be self-effacing?

Your face glows like a heated lamp but still
What do you know of the joy of melting in the heat of passion?

When has he bowed and begged in dire indigence?
How can Sheikh saheb know of prayer and its essence?

Once he has stepped on the road of real love
What does he care if he sinks to the bottom or rises high above?

Ask the wine drinkers to tell you of the delights of wine
What do the virtuous know of its pleasures divine?

She who does not know her own heart till today
What will she know of my heart and its state?

Hazrat Khizr has no acquaintance with death[167]
How can he know then the felicity of a long life?

What all calamities befall Daagh
How would my friends and benefactors realise?

Allah! Allah! That soft velvety hour, that small voice and the tone to melt the heart, the words and their supremely artful patterns, and most of all, Daagh's boyishly simple face, all combined to create a rare magnetism. There was nobody in the mehfil who did not lose himself in the aura; there was nobody who was not spontaneously exclaiming, Jazak-allah or Subhan-allah or Salle-'alaa. Mirza Fakhru was secretly enjoying all of the praise. He changed sides from time to time, and it was easy to see his heart

---

[167]In the Quran, in Surah al-Kahf, there is a story wherein Moses encounters the mysterious servant and esoteric figure, who is not named, but who is identified by commentators and by a Hadith of the Prophet as Hazrat Khizr or Khidr (or al-Khidr, the 'Green One'). Moses meets Khizr at the junction of the two seas, at which point the two prophets, one representing exoteric knowledge (Moses) and the other esoteric (Khizr), journey together briefly. Khizr is considered to be kept alive by God beyond the range of human life, and even beyond the very long lifetimes of certain ancient prophets like Noah. But his vocation is secret and hidden.

In Sufism, Khizr is considered the prophet of initiation into divine mysteries as well as a special spiritual guide from whom many claim to have received initiation, including the famous Sufi metaphysician Ibn-Arabi.

Seyyed Hossein Nasr, *The Study Quran: A New Translation and Commentary*, pp. 729, 748.

swelling with pride. The ghazal wove to its end, but nobody noticed that it had ended. Only when the lamp reached Hakim Momin Khan Momin did their excitement subside somewhat, and they became attentive again in anticipation of the recitation by the ustad of rekhta.

Hakim Momin Khan lifted the lamp and placed it away from himself, a little ahead of where it had been. Then he straightened up and ran his fingers through his hair in the manner of a comb, adjusted his cap to be at an angle, picked consciously at the pleats of his sleeves and finally began reading his ghazal in a sensitive and stirring tone.

ulTe voh shikve karte haiN aur kis adaa ke saath
be-taaqatii ke taane haiN uzr-e-jafaa ke saath

bahr-e-ayaadat aaye voh lekin qazaa ke saath
dam hi nikal gaya mira aavaaz-e paa ke saath

maaNga kareNge ab se dua hijr-e-yaar ki
aaKHir to dushmani hai asar ko dua ke saath

hai kis ka intezaar ke KHaab-e-adam se bhi
har baar chauNk paDte haiN aavaaz-e-paa ke saath

sau zindagi nisaar karuN aisi maut par
yuN roye zaar-zaar to ahl-e-azaa ke saath

be-pardaa Gair paas use baiTHa na dekhte
uTH jaate kaash hum bhi jahaaN se hayaa ke saath

uski gali kahaaN, yeh to kuchh baaG-e KHuld hai
kis jaay mujh ko chhoD gai maut la ke saath

Allah re gumrahi! but-o-butKHana chhoD kar
Momin chalaa hai Kaa'be ko ik paarsaa ke saath

She quibbles unfairly and so charmingly
Taunts me of being powerless, to inflict gentle cruelty

She came to ask about my well-being upon my end
It took my life, the sound of her approaching steps

From now on, my dua will be for separation from the beloved
After all, well known is the enmity between prayer and its fulfilment

Who do I wait for even in the nether world of death?
Every time I get startled at the sound of footsteps

I would gladly give up a hundred lives for such a death
Her tears overflow copiously as everyone mourns my ceased breath

If only I had not seen her seated casually with a stranger
If only I had left the world before experiencing such dishonour

What is this? Not her lane, nay, this is some Garden of Eden
Where has Death left me after bringing me from the world of men?

Allah re, you lost one! Turning away from the temple and false gods
Momin is headed to the Holy Kaa'ba with a virtuous soul.

Was it a ghazal or a spell? The entire mehfil sat in a state of total absorption, entranced. Momin Khan himself was exulting in his words. While reading a sher he particularly relished, his fingers would twist brightly through his hair; as the intensity heightened, his fingers tangled and twirled the curls on his head with greater speed. When somebody expressed appreciation for a sher, he acknowledged it with an imperceptible nod of his head and a faint shadow of a smile. His reading was quite unique. His hands moved only the slightest bit—but then, his hands were also not available, busy as they were with his locks. With the up-and-down intonation of his voice and with fluid gestures of his eyes, he spun a force field of sheer magic. Upon the completion of the ghazal, the masters were full of glowing praise. He smiled and responded, 'It is your graciousness! All my hard work has been rewarded. I have already said,

hum daad ke KHaahaaN haiN, nahiiN talab-e-zar kuchh
tehsiin-e-sukhan fahm hai, Momin, silaa apna

I wish for appreciation, it's not any riches I seek
Praise from the knowing and discerning, Momin, is my reward.'

After him, the lamp went to Ustad Ehsaan. I had thought that his voice would barely reach anyone, but as soon as the lamp reached him, he changed colour and became someone else entirely. His voice became loud and strong, and the ghazal he recited was a great hit with the mehfil.

In his reading of the ghazal, he engaged with his peers in that inimitable manner of master poets, who have over time, accrued an abundance of understanding of one another's poetry and persona, and who spontaneously seek their approbation. For one sher, he addressed Momin Khan; for another, he directed his gaze to Mirza Nausha; for yet another, he turned towards Ustad Zauq. His eminence was well acknowledged by all, and every master he addressed his sher to was impelled to voice his appreciation fulsomely. The radiif was difficult and the qafiya was tricky, but despite these, his masterful working of the language was indeed praiseworthy and his ghazal came studded with aural gems.

tu kyuN hai giryaa kunaaN ai mere dil-e mahzuuN
na ro na ro, ke na tujhko kabhi rulaye Khuda

butoN! bataao to, kya tum Khuda ko doge javaab?
Khuda ke bandoN pe yeh zulm, banda haai Khuda!

razaa pe teri hoN din raat sanam masruuf
jo is pe tu nahiiN raazi, na ho, razaa-e Khuda

butoN ke kuche meiN kehta tha kal yehi Ehsaan
yahaaN kisii ka nahiiN hai koi sivaay Khuda

O my aggrieved heart! Why do you wail brokenly thus?
Weep not, may the Almighty never give you reason to moan thus

O idols! Tell me, what answer will you give to God?
Torturing God's creatures like this, O creatures of God!

May the nights and days obey you, beloved!
If you don't concede to it, don't, it is as God wills

Ehsaan was saying in the lane of the idols yesterday
There's nobody for anyone in this world other than Khuda.

When he had concluded, it was Mirza Ghalib's turn. This was in a new light. Dawn was stealing over the city in fragile threads of pink and grey that cut through the night and replaced its dark mood with a lively mellifluousness. When the lamp came before Mirza Ghalib, he said, 'Good sirs! I will also now sing my Bhairavi alaap.'[168] So saying, he read his ghazal in a magnificently melting tone, and the mehfil was elated. His recitation voice was loud and laden with emotion. It was as if he had no allies or friends here, and he was entreating them with his seductive words to win their hearts.

dil-e-naadaN! tujhe hua kya hai?
aKHir is dard ki davaa kya hai?

[168]In Hindustani classical music, raags have an associated time of day when they are meant to be sung or played. Raag Bhairavi is an early morning raag and is sung to herald the start of a new day, therefore Mirza Ghalib's apt mention.

hum haiN mushtaaq aur voh bezaar
ya ilahi! yeh maajra kya hai!

maiN bhi muNh meiN zabaan rakhta huN
kaash puchho ke muddaa' kya hai?

jab ke tujh bin nahiiN koi maujuud
phir yeh hangaamaa ai Khuda kya hai?

yeh pari chehra log kaise haiN?
Gamza-o-ishvah-o-adaa kya hai?

shikan-e-zulf-e ambariiN kyuN hai?
nigah-e chashm-e surma sa kya hai?

hum ko unse vafaa ki hai ummiid
jo nahiiN jaante vafaa kya hai

haaN bhalaa kar tera bhalaa hoga
aur darvesh ki sadaa kya hai!

jaan tum par nisaar karta huN
maiN nahiiN jaanta dua kya hai

maine maanaa ki kuchh nahiiN Ghalib
muft haath aaye to buraa kya hai!

My foolish heart! What has happened to you?
What is the cure for this malady that ails you?

Here I am overcome with passion and she remains unmoved
Ya Ilaahi! What on earth is the matter with you?

I too have a tongue, I too can speak
If only someone would ask, 'What's the matter with you?'

When indeed only you exist and no one else
What then, O God, is this grand fuss about You?

Who are these people with their bright angel faces?
What for is all their coquetry and charm and lure?

Why these tresses with waves and curls fragrant like amber?
What looks like kohl in those eyes gazing at you?

My vain hope that she will return my love and trust
She who knows nothing of faithfulness in love to you

Do good and the good will come back to you
What more does the wandering dervish call out to you!

I will give my life for you without a second thought
What do I know of prayer and praying for you?

I acknowledge that Ghalib is worth nothing at all
If he comes at no cost what's the loss to you!

After reading his ghazal he smiled and quipped, 'Now if she does not understand even after this, then may God deal with her!'

Hakim Aaga Jaan was quick to grasp the allusion to his earlier remark about Ghalib's poetry being understood only by Ghalib himself or by God. He said, 'Mirza saheb, thank God, at long last you have understood this colour of life!' In short, there were accolades for Mirza Ghalib's ineffable genius, and at the same time, good-natured jesting, as would be expected among equals.

In the meantime, the lamp came to Ustad Zauq. Ustad Zauq looked towards Mirza Fakhru and asked, 'Saheb-e-alam, should I read a ghazal or a qata I composed yesterday? Last night, God knows what it was, but I wasn't able to get to sleep no matter how much I tried. I spent the entire night twisting and turning until finally it was dawn. I savoured the mood of a shab-e-hijr, a night of separation! In that fevered state, a qata came to me. With your leave, I'd like to read it.'

Mirza Fakhru replied, 'Ustad, today's mushaira is free of all constraints. You can read a ghazal or you can read a qasidah or a rubai or qata, you can read whatever your heart desires. Only, do read something!'

Ustad Zauq prepared himself to read his qata and then recited in a forceful voice that reverberated in the gathering. His distinctive manner compounded the effect of his words of pain and puzzlement.[169]

kahuN kya Zauq! ahvaal-e shab-e-hijr
ke thi ik-ik ghaDi sau-sau mahiine

na thi shab, Daal rakkha thaa ik andher
mere baKHt-e siyeh ki tiirgii ne

tap-e-Gam shama-saaN hoti na thi kam
aur aate the pasiinoN par pasiine

yehi kahta thaa ghabra kar falak se
ke O be-mehr bad-aKHtar kamiine!

kahaaN maiN aur kahaaN yeh sab, magar the
mire jaanib se tire dil meiN kiine

sau is zulmat ke parde meiN kiye zulm
arre zaalim! tiri kiina-vari ne

ivaz kis baadaanoshi ke, mujhe aaj
paDe yeh zahr ke se ghuunT piine

havaas-o-hosh jo mujh se qariiN the
qariine se hue sab be-qariine

miri siina-zanii ka shor sun kar
phaTe jaate the hum-saayoN ke siine

---

[169] Azad writes in part seven of *Aab-e hayat*, 'When he (Ustad Zauq) recited in a mushaira, the gathering would echo. His style of reciting gave the emotional effect of his poetry even more force. He himself recited his own ghazals. He absolutely never gave them to anyone else to recite.' *https://dsal.uchicago.edu/books/PK2155.H8413/442457d5.html*

uTHaya gaah aur gaahe baiTHaya
mujhe betaabi-o-betaaqati ne

kahaa jab dil ne, tu kuchh khaa ke so reh
bohat almaas ke toDe nagiine

na TuuTaa jaan ka qaalib se rishta
bohat hi jaan toDi jaaN-kanii ne

bohat dekha na dikhlaya zaraa bhi
talva-e-sub.h se muNh roshni ne

kaha jii ne mujhe yeh hijr ki raat
yaqiiN hai sub.h tak degi na jiine

lage paani chuvaane muNh meiN aaNsuu
paDHi yaasiin sirhaane be-kasii ne

magar din umr ke thoDe se baaqii
lagaa rakkhe the miri zindagii ne

ke qismat se qariib-e-KHana mire
azaaN masjid meiN dii baare kisii ne

bashaarat mujh ko sub.h-e vasl ki dii
azaaN ke saath yumn-o-farruKHi ne

hui aisi KHushi Allah-o-Akbar!
ke KHush ho kar kahaa yeh KHud KHushi ne

mo'azzan marhabaa! bar-o-qat bola
tiri aavaaz Makke aur Madiine

What should I say Zauq of the night of parting?
Every instant stretched into a hundred months

It was not night, but a black cloak thrown over me
Of gloom ushered by a dark stroke of fate

Like a lighted candle, the heat of anguish would not abate
And beads of sweat formed on my brow layer upon layer

In desperation I hurled accusations at the skies
At the tired-out sun, stars of the evil eye

I am here, and you are far on high, and still
You nurse ill will for me in your heart

You have committed a hundred tyrannies
With the malice you bear towards me

For the crime of drinking wine
Today I have to swallow this bowl of poison

My ever-present sense and sensibility have
Very neatly scattered into chaos tonight

Upon hearing the tortured clamour of my beating heart
The hearts of my neighbours split open with pain

I was impelled to stand up and sit down again and again
By bouts of impatience and impotence of limbs in vain

Whispered my heart, 'Swallow something and get to sleep'
And I emptily crumbled verse-diamonds into gems

The soul resisted to break loose from the frame
Even as a rigour mortis-stiffness came over my limbs

I looked hard but could not find even a remote sign
Of first light on the thin edge of day

My heart was convinced this night of parting
Would not let me live to see a new day

Tears dripped water into my mouth, as when dying
Someone recited Surah Ya-Sin by my head[170]

---

[170]Several scholars maintain that the *Surah Ya-Sin* is 'The Heart of the Quran'

Even so a few days of my journey remain
Lined up by my life ever awake

Coincidentally just then in the masjid close by
Someone called the azaan for the fajr namaaz[171]

Gave me tidings of the dawn of coming together
With the azaan, the benediction of joy and prosperity

I felt a deep surge of elation, Allah-o-Akbar
And joy itself proclaimed with delight,

Praise be to the muezzin who called just in time!
Your call echoed in Mecca and Medina!

Just as the last sher was read, it was time for the morning prayer. From the nearby masjid came the cadence of the call to the worshippers. 'Allah-o-Akbar! Allah-o-Akbar! Allah-o-Akbar! Allah-o-Akbar!' Automatically, everyone murmured: 'Your call echoed in Mecca and Medina!'

As the call to prayer gently fell away, everyone in the gathering raised their hands for dua, after which Mirza Fakhru said, 'Sirs! What a fortunate coincidence that the mushaira began with the Fatiha Khair and ends too with the Fatiha Khair.' With these words, he bent forward and extinguished the two lamps that had been brought back to him after their respective circulations in the mehfil. As soon as the lamps were put out, the heralds called out, 'Hazraat! The mushaira is now over.'

At these words, everyone stood up to go home. Mirza Fakhru

---

because it addresses its central teachings regarding God, prophethood and the Hereafter. It is recited for those who are sick or close to death, or those who have just died and also at the grave of a loved one. Many Muslims also recite *Ya-Sin* regularly as a part of their supererogatory devotions.

Seyyed Hossein Nasr, *The Study Quran: A New Translation and Commentary*, p. 1069.

[171]Fajr namaaz is the first prayer of the day before the sun rises.

was the first to get into his palanquin and leave. Thereafter, one by one, everyone began to troop out. In the end only Nawab Zain ul-Abidin Khan and I were left. I turned and expressed an earnest shukriya to him.

He replied, 'Miyaan Karimuddin! This is the result of your good intentions that the mushaira went off without any difficulty and in fact, so smoothly. Your work has also been done and I got what my heart desired. Khuda hafiz then!'

My fate

darmaandgii meiN Ghalib kuchh ban paDe to jaanuN
jab rishta be-girah thaa naKHuun girah-kusha thaa

If only I could do something, Ghalib, in my misfortune
When the bond was knot-free, my nails were sharp
enough to undo any knot.

The next day, everything that had been brought to the house for the mushaira was taken away. Once again, it was the old familiar home, with the rhythmic clatter of the printing press and its troubles. The next month, I again announced a mushaira and printed and distributed advertisements for it. Unfortunately, only a handful of people turned up for it, and ultimately after a few months, I stopped organising the mushaira.

It was a difficult time for me, as I suffered losses. A few of my employees failed to pay back the advances I had given them. Then after a few weeks, my partners cheated me and took control of my press. I was quite helpless. I thought if I appealed to a court of law, I would get justice and things could be set right. But then I got distracted by other events that overtook my life, and never got around to taking the legal route.

The poetry manuscript from that fateful mushaira is still with me. Let's see when it gets published and who publishes it.

Appendix A

Rasheed Hasan Khan's preface (1991)

You will read an account of a mushaira held in 1261 AH (1845) in the forthcoming pages. The way in which the fine details of this mushaira have been presented makes the reader believe that the mushaira was held just like this. As a matter of fact, Mirza Farhatullah Baig has himself written at the beginning that indeed, he arranged the mehfil in this fashion as per his understanding.

Maulvi Karimuddin belonged to Panipat, but he had made Dehli his home. He completed his education here. He wrote several books, and one of the most famous is a tazkirah of Urdu poets called *Tab'qat-e shora-e Hind*. In this tazkirah, he mentions a mushaira that used to be held at his home. 'This mushaira at my house started on 14 Rajab 1261 AH. In the same year, it was discontinued during the month of Zii-qaa'd.'[172] Karimuddin also clarifies that Nawab Zain ul-Abidin Khan Arif used to be the Mir-e-mushaira. Where he has mentioned Arif in the tazkirah, he writes, 'In the duration when the mushaira used to be held at my printing press, this very poet was designated as Mir-e-majlis and Mir-e-mushaira.'

In this way, Farhatullah Baig got a clue for a mushaira, of which Arif used to be Mir-e-mushaira. On the basis of these

[172]Rajab is the seventh month in the Islamic calendar, while Zii-qaa'd, the eleventh.

two sketchy facts, he pieced together the portrait of a mehfil in which he brought together the legendary poets of Dehli along with the not-so-famous poets. In doing so, his aim was to keep the memory of that epoch evergreen in people's hearts and to impress on people's minds, the images of the poets of that time. He states all this at the start of the essay in adequate detail:

> I found a word-sketch of Hakim Momin Khan 'Momin' Dehlvi in some ancient documents. And no sooner had I found this, than an idea bubbled up in my mind that like Muhammad Husain Azad's mehfil of poets in his *Nairang-e khayaal*, I too should institute a mushaira...I should faithfully mirror the poets' walking and talking pictures...I felt deeply moved to light a lamp for Urdu from their lights, to be able to illuminate this age for coming generations. I felt that future Urdu lovers should catch a glimpse of these last titans far from their time, however hazy it might be. I felt it was important to show the readers, the dead poets' faces and expressions as they recited.

Mirza Farhatullah Baig belonged to Dehli, but went to Hyderabad in 1907 in search of employment. He lived there throughout his life and died on 27 April 1947. And so, through his working life, until his last breath, he stayed in Hyderabad. But his writings clearly show that he never forgot his city Dehli. The luminous shadows of Dehli's literary and cultural life stayed alight in his heart. As the poet says:

miT gaye voh nazaare, haai jamiil
lekin aakhoN meiN aks chhoD gaye

Those delightful scenes are alas, no more
But they left behind their reflection in the eyes.

Mirza saheb's fame rests on his special flair as a humorist and sketch-writer. There's no doubt that he was a sketch-writer of the highest order. His biographical sketch of his teacher, Maulvi Nazeer Ahmad, is much more than a sketch—it has assumed a life-sized form filled with light, and can be seen from afar, walking and talking. Several sketches have been written in Urdu, and by accomplished writers too, but to find a sketch close to this is difficult and most difficult indeed. And there's a reason for that.

Mirza saheb was not only a prose writer, he was also a painter and a dramatist. He had a deep love for these arts. Not only was he writing plays, he also had a deep love for acting. One of the essayists of *Yaadgaar-e Farhat*, Mirza Asmatullah Baig writes, 'Marhoom (Farhatullah Baig) had an instinctive love for playwriting and acting. By chance an English actor, Heming, travelled to Dehli. Farhatullah immediately became his shagird... He was fond of painting and art and was also a pupil of Dehli's well-known and celebrated artist Ustad Arif.'

Baig wrote a script for a film too, it's another matter that it could not get made into a film. Himanshu Rai, the famous film-maker of his time, asked Baig to make some changes that he felt were essential from a film-making perspective. Mirza saheb was not agreeable to this and as a result, the project got stalled. In 1951, the Farhat Memorial Committee published a book, *Yaadgaar-e Farhat*; included in this collection is an essay by Mirza saheb's cousin brother, Mirza Rafiq Baig, that has the details. And yes, he (Farhatullah Baig) also wrote poetry.

Baig's great love for painting, playwriting and acting and their influence on his craft breathed waves of life into the sketch he wrote of Maulvi Nazeer Ahmad. Regardless of the exceptional quality of Maulvi Nazeer Ahmad saheb's biographical word-sketch, it stays very much within the traditional framework of a savaanihi khaaka, a biographical sketch, and that is truly remarkable. In comparison, the narration of Dehli's last mushaira has taken the form of a muraqqa', a word picture, and in this, Baig's talent and skill in painting and playwriting leave their imprint conspicuously. To say this is an account of a mushaira would be restricting, because as the reader goes through it, it feels as if the poets are seated right before the reader, laughing and talking amongst themselves, having conversations, reciting their verses. There is no single person who stands out in prominent relief; every person is recognisable by his singular attributes and special traits. Every character is life-like and real. In present-day terms, it is a one-act play.

The element of drama begins with the way Mirza saheb has presented Nawab Zain ul-Abidin Khan Arif. In Karimuddin's tazkirah, Nawab Arif is generally Mir-e-mushaira for all mushairas. Mirza Farhatullah put an end to this generality; this was necessary. The grand scale of the mehfil that Mirza saheb wanted to depict—Maulvi Karimuddin was not apt for it. How could the princes of Qila-e-Mu'alla and Dehli's famous teachers have gathered upon Karimuddin's invitation, and why would Mirza Fakhru attend the mushaira? Forget about inviting these people, even picturing all these personalities together was quite beyond the ambit of Maulvi Karimuddin's thought and vision. Mirza Farhatullah Baig was keenly aware of this, and so he made Nawab Arif the principal character, on the weight of whose name distinguished people could be gathered at one place, and who was capable of arranging a magnificent mehfil fit for the royals.

As a result of the dramatic elements present in this mushaira, it can be successfully enacted on stage, and has indeed been staged. The mushaira was staged for the first time by Maulvi Abdul Haq on the occasion of Aurangabad College Day at Aurangabad. And Mirza Farhatullah Baig was himself the stage director. Mirza Asmatullah Baig writes, 'The imaginary had been made real!'

Superficially it is a mushaira, but in reality, upon reading it, glimpses of the literary and cultural life of the Dehli of that era are seen. The mushaira that was attended by the rulers from the Qila—how it was laid out, how the various poets were made to be seated and in what manner, how appreciation was given in the mushaira, how the great ustads would give praise and recite their verses, the manner of arrangements that were necessary for a good mushaira, all these things are seen. It is also learnt that the mushaira of the time was not just a gathering for reciting poetry, it had a cultural status. Think of the mushairas we see today; then, upon reading about this mushaira, we can guess why there is the stark difference of night and day between mushairas then and now.

In this mushaira, Mirza saheb has included all types of poets from across all social classes and the key outcome of this is that the gathering has retained its colour and variety. The character of Meer saheb comes forth, therefore, as extraordinarily heartwarming and lighted up with a lively theatrical quality. Such characters are to be found in every era, in some form or the other.

Mirza saheb, with his superb storytelling, has laid out the narrative in all its rich detail in a way that Meer saheb's presence relieves the monotony of the recitation. The Meer saheb interlude gives a brief reprieve to both the poets and the readers' minds to refresh themselves and then get ready to relish the verses again and revel in the poetry of the ustads. On the other hand, great care has been exercised to ensure that not a single sentence is uttered that is not befitting for a mehfil adorned by the presence of Mirza Fakhru and that also has in attendance the great revered teachers. Not only the ustads, erudite and well-known scholars like Maulvi Mamluk-ul Ali and Maulana Sehbai also participate in the jesting give-and-take (with Meer saheb). Whether objections or questions and answers, the intention is to create a light-hearted diversion and to change the atmosphere of the mehfil for a brief interval. But even this wholly entertaining banter is not sans an intellectual hue. The kind of mehfil it is, the level of the people gathered, the light-hearted interregnum is of a matching shade and of an appropriate level. The scholarship is of a fine hue, and the lighter side no less; what's more, not even a shadow can be found of any triteness or banality.

One thing we must keep in mind about the mushaira. It is true that Mirza saheb has described a mushaira held in 1261 AH at Maulvi Karimuddin's place, but it does not mean that Mirza saheb has portrayed that particular mushaira itself. Like a good storyteller and dramatist, he has used that mushaira only as a central core. If he had not depicted this mushaira and if he had not made it his cornerstone; if Mirza Farhatullah had simply put together a mehfil for a mushaira after his own fashion, irrespective of how expertly he filled that portrait with real colours, it would still have been a 'khayaali' mehfil, a gathering he had thought up. It would have tones of storytelling and fiction narration, but it would not be lighted up with realism. A good example of this is Muhammad Husain Azad assembling a similar mehfil in his work, *Nairang-e khayaal*, and bringing together poets and men of knowledge. Azad was a peerless prose writer, adept at depicting imaginary assemblies and animating words into living pictures, and nobody could equal him in his skill with crafting poetry and telling stories. Despite all these remarkable distinctions, Azad's mehfil appears like a thing of imagination. In contrast, Mirza saheb's mushaira looks like a real mushaira. A key reason for this difference is that Mirza saheb centred his storied mushaira on a real mushaira that had actually been held. Of course, the real mushaira had been a small affair, whereas Mirza saheb's mehfil embraces the entire period; it encompasses the literary life of the Dehli of the time, bringing it vibrantly alive on his canvas.

The reader's attention has been especially drawn to the fact that it's not necessary to apply the yardstick of rigour in research for the poets who have been assembled and whose kalaam has been presented. This is not a critical essay or a scholarly research-based treatise. This is also not a historical work. This is only an attempt, and a very successful attempt, to present a pen-portrait of the famous poets of that era that can aid present-day students to gain familiarity with the poets' personalities, their style and attitude, and their rhythm and mode of poetry presentation. This has been enunciated by Mirza Farhatullah himself at the start of the essay.

People with an intellectual affinity know that to show the dead poets' faces and expressions as they recited, their movements of hands and eyes, delightful lyrical cadences, the dramatic pauses and play in their reciting voices, noting how they sat down or rose from their seats, their persona and manner, and most significantly, the poets' typical dress and style—all these have the power to create a deep imaginative space of enchantment for readers and enhance their reading experience twice over.

At one time, mushairas were a manifestation of our cultural life. Today, mushairas have been reduced to a form of entertainment or a means of spending or earning money. Present-day students, upon reading this account of an old-style mushaira, will be able to easily compare the old with the new. Along with this, they will also be able to learn that a mushaira was not just a gathering for poetry recitation; it mirrored the tehzeeb of the time—the etiquette and protocol of the mehfil, the manner in which it was organised, everything it encompassed. Even today, a mushaira mirrors the tehzeeb of the present time, but the difference between the ethos of the past and the present is clearly highlighted. A lot of such things are not found in history books also, and therefore, such essays have immense value.

This essay of Mirza Farhatullah Baig (it should be called a literary and cultural portrait) was first published in the journal, *Urdu*, of Anjuman Taraqqi Urdu (Hind)[173] in 1927. M. Jeb Khan

[173]The journal *Urdu* was first published in 1921 from Hyderabad, India, by the-then General Secretary, Maulvi Abdul Haq. He moved to Pakistan at the time of the Partition in 1947 and began publishing *Urdu* there. Meanwhile, Anjuman Taraqqi Urdu (Hind) shifted its office to Aligarh, and in 1951, it started publishing the

saheb kindly provided me with the photocopy of that edition from the Anjuman library. It was also included in the first part of *Mazameen-e Farhat* (first edition, Hyderabad). Upon examination, it was found that while including the essay in *Mazameen-e Farhat*, Mirza Farhatullah Baig saheb had made some revisions in it. On that basis, I have used the text in *Mazameen-e Farhat* for this edition. It is also a fact that in this book, requisite emendations have been made with the help of the essay included in the journal *Urdu*. This essay has been published under various names. Khwaja Hasan Nizami had published this under the title *Dehli ki aakhri shama*, but Mirza Farhatullah Baig had called it *1261* AH *mein Dehli ka ek mushaira*, and this is the title that has been maintained.

Rasheed Hasan Khan
18 October 1991

---

journal *Urdu Adab*, adding 'Adab' to the original name to differentiate it from the journal by the Anjuman Taraqqi Urdu Pakistan. The first editor for *Urdu Adab* was Ale Ahmad Suroor, who later also became the General Secretary.

Appendix B
Sketches of master poets

Mirza Asadullah Khan Ghalib (1797–1869)

Mirza Asadullah Khan Ghalib was born on 27 December 1797 CE in Agra. When he was four or five years old, his father died in a skirmish while in the service of the king of Alwar. Asadullah was then put in the care of his uncle, his father's brother, who served with the Marathas and rose to be the commander of Agra Fort. Soon after, his uncle too fell to his death from an elephant's back. Asadullah was nine years old then. Ultimately, he and his brother were raised by his mother and maternal grandparents. His mother's family was well-placed in Agra and Ghalib had a happy, almost privileged childhood in spite of his early losses.

Ghalib's initial education was at home, and it's possible that he attended a madrasa for a few months. Details of his later education are not known. In 1810, at the age of thirteen, he was married to eleven-year-old Umrao Begum, the niece of the Nawab of Loharu and Ferozepur Jhirka. Umrao's father, Mirza Ilahi Bakhsh Khan, was an influential jagirdar and the younger brother of the Nawab of Loharu. Ghalib came to be called Nausha miyaan ('nausha' meaning bridegroom in Urdu) after his marriage and the moniker stuck throughout his life. The couple moved to Delhi a year after their marriage and made it their home for the rest of their lives.

Ghalib and Umrao were an unusual couple. Ghalib was an easy-going and free-spirited man of the world. He loved the company of his friends and fellow poets. A man of many parts, he remained greater than the sum of them all, and a literary enigma for the ages. His love for the finer things, his penchant for expensive liquor and his craving for mangoes are amply documented. He is equally well known for his dismissive attitude towards ritualised religious practice. His poetic oeuvre remains a subject of ongoing joyous discovery, as each succeeding generation of poets and scholars peels away yet another layer of time, uncovering new facets and drawing forth hitherto-unseen pearls.

Umrao, on the other hand, was homely, God-fearing and punctiliously observant. The couple had seven children but they all died either during childbirth or in infancy. Over time, this void became a festering wound for them both. There was the additional burden of looking after Ghalib's younger brother who suffered from schizophrenia, and the latter's family. Financial difficulties dogged the household unceasingly. Umrao turned to her religion, Ghalib to his social life and poetry. It is no secret that Mirza could never, right through his life, fully attune himself to domestic entrapments.

Ghalib began writing at an early age and wrote in Persian. His Persian ustad remains a hazy figure in history, supposedly an Iranian teacher named Abdul Samad, who was visiting Agra from Iran, and who stayed at Ghalib's grandfather's home for about two years. It is his Urdu poetry, however, that earned Ghalib a monumental reputation for all time to come.

He lived and breathed poetry, undoubtedly, but Mirza Ghalib was also an inveterate letter writer who wrote frequent and vivid letters to his friends, providing illuminating insights into his life and his city. The letters, written in conversational Urdu and peppered with his trademark dry humour, not only reveal the changing seasons of his heart and mind, they are also a testimony to the changing hues of his time. Present-day scholars ascribe the same literary value to his letters as they do to his poetry.

Despite all the challenges, Mirza kept up a cheerful facade and derived solace from his friends and students. Muhammad Husain Azad, a young student-poet during Ghalib's time, elucidates on this aspect of his personality:

> Mirza had a large number of friends. He was such a true friend to his friends that he cherished them more than most people do their relatives. His love of his friends, accompanied by his sunny temper, constantly kept him surrounded by a circle of nobles and the elite. Through them he diverted his grief, and in this was his life. The most interesting part is that he spoke to his friends' sons in just the same way as to his friends. For their part, promising young men would sit with respect. For his part, he would shower them with the flowers of mature witticisms. For their part, the well-behaved boys would smile and say nothing, and if they spoke, they never took a step beyond the bounds of courtesy. For his part, he still didn't leave off his liveliness of temperament. All this created an extraordinary atmosphere. In any case, through his jests and witticisms he took his mind off the difficulties of the time. And turning the unpleasant into the pleasant, he went on his way, laughing and amusing himself.[174]

Financial difficulties were the weft of Ghalib's life right until his death. His luckless endeavours to gain control of the money that the British government owed his family is the stuff of endless stories. He stubbornly persisted, writing letters upon letters to the British Resident and others in the government. His claim remained stuck in the labyrinth of British officialdom with its constantly shifting coordinates of what constituted a legitimate pension claim with regard to Indian elites and who was a rightful

[174] Azad, *Aab-e hayat, https://dsal.uchicago.edu/books/PK2155.H8413/481499d5.html*

claimant. Sometime towards the end of 1826 or in early 1827, he undertook a long drawn out, arduous trip to Calcutta in order to make a stronger and personalised appeal for his pension. Once there, he called on the Assistant and the Chief Secretary and had cordial meetings with them. Ghalib finally returned to Delhi in August 1829. Unsurprisingly, his pension claim was later rejected.

The end result of Mirza's Calcutta sojourn may have been bitterly disappointing, but a pleasant byproduct was his passage through various north Indian cities like Kanpur, Lucknow, Benaras, Allahabad and towns like Murshidabad. With Benaras, it was love at first sight; Ghalib was enchanted. He immortalised the ancient city in a masnavi, *Chirag-e-dair* (*Lamp of the Temple*), and raved about it as the 'Kaa'ba of Hindustan'. Calcutta too, left its mark, captivating him with its vivid greenery, its superb wines and not least, the charming Bengali women.

While in Calcutta, Ghalib was invited to attend a mushaira where he read two ghazals in Persian before a large gathering. A few in the gathering raised objections on some of his constructions, and Ghalib was stung to the quick to be censured for the very language he considered his forte. The incident blew up into an unpleasant affair. But aside from this unnecessary controversy that simmered for a while, Ghalib got a unique opportunity to observe at close quarters the modern developments in the British-ruled city. He saw the impact of the printing press that had still to come to Delhi, the translation of English classics into Urdu at Fort William College, and more. He noted how technological advancement accelerated social change. The world was changing before his eyes, and Ghalib took it all in enthusiastically.

Amar Farooqui writes:

> Syed Ahmed Khan had requested Ghalib for a laudatory foreword (taqriz), as was then the literary convention, for his forthcoming publication. …In the taqriz, composed in verse,

> Ghalib marvels at the way in which the power of steam has been tamed, at the speed with which the telegraph makes news travel, at civic amenities such as street lighting ('Go to London, for in that shining garden / The city is bright in the night without candles').[175]

In the early 1840s, Ghalib was offered a professorship in Persian at the Delhi College, the Mecca of a modern style education attracting students from across the country. But the transaction did not unfold to Mirza's satisfaction and his sense of personal prestige, and eventually, he refused the offer. In any case, a salaried job at the college was still a new concept for a poet. And Ghalib firmly believed that with his lineage and credentials, he richly merited royal patronage, such that it would give him the freedom to craft a literary legacy without having to worry about the banal business of earning a livelihood. Royal patronage eventually came, but by then, it was worth little.

Then in 1847, the poet was arrested for gambling. This was a time when the British were passionately evangelising a new morality and had taken upon themselves the responsibility of reforming those Indian habits and social ills that they judged as being 'immoral'. A hostile kotwal and a newly-appointed stiff-necked magistrate, unaware of Ghalib's social station, sentenced him to six months of imprisonment and a fine. The judgment was unkind and unfair, and it shocked not just Ghalib, but all of Delhi. The Mughal Emperor intervened to seek some relief for the beleaguered poet, but the British officials were in no mood to show any clemency. Ghalib ended up spending three months in prison, after which he was released. But it was the summer season and he suffered; although greater than the physical distress was the humiliation of being put away in the manner of a common criminal. In spite of being a great personal setback, however, the

[175] Amar Farooqui, *Zafar and the Raj: Anglo-Mughal Delhi c. 1800-1850*, p.121.

prison sentence did not in any way dent his fame as a poet. Delhi-wallahs knew full well that Mirza Nausha was hardly a criminal to have been incarcerated thus, and the incident was only an affirmation of the inflexibility and whimsical nature of the firangi administration. And there was nothing anybody could do about it, not even the Mughal Badshah!

Around this time, Ghalib got increased access to the Mughal court. This might have been thanks to his close friends Hakim Ahsanullah Khan, who was the Emperor's physician and close confidant, and Kaale saheb, Bahadur Shah's spiritual guide. In 1850 at long last, Zafar bestowed upon Ghalib the titles of Najam-ud-Daula, Dabir-ul-mulk and Nizam Jang. The Mughal Badshah also commissioned him to write a history of the Timurid dynasty at six hundred rupees per year. It's another matter the project was never completed.

Between Zafar and Ghalib, there slowly grew a mutually respectful relationship, and over time, it matured into easy informality. It helped shore up the poet's social position. When Ustad Zauq died in 1854, Ghalib was appointed as Zafar's ustad. Still, the official title of Malik-ush-Shora (Poet Laureate) eluded him. By now, unfortunately, there was no financial benefit to be expected from the position, given the depleted state of the Mughal treasury, and Ghalib was fairly unenthusiastic about it. What's more, it was too late in the day; Ghalib could never forget that he had not been the Badshah's first choice for teacher.

As the Badshah's ustad, Ghalib was expected to be present at the Qila every day and his schedule turned out to be quite taxing. After a full day, he was also expected to join the Badshah for leisure activities like kite flying or simply a walk in the garden. But there were perks too. The two men genuinely enjoyed each other's company. Between them, there was respect and reserve, a subtle intimacy, warmth and a generous sprinkling of light-hearted poetic humour as among equals. Altaf Husain Hali[176] narrates an incident when Ghalib gushed over the delicious mangoes in the royal orchard and the Emperor promptly had a basket of the fruit sent to his home. Both were men of the world and both knew full well that they were witness to a passing summer. And thus did the years pass for the poet, now past his prime.

Then came the summer of 1857, and with it came uncertainty, fear and struggle for the very soul of Ghalib's beloved Delhi. When the Indian troops landed unannounced at Delhi's doorstep that fateful morning in May, Ghalib's future became inextricably linked with the fate of the city. His letters tell of the systematic plunder and destruction of Delhi, the terrorising of its unsuspecting populace, first at the hands of the rebel Indian troops and later by the British army. He was profoundly pained at the brutalities brazenly unleashed on ordinary citizens. It was also his unfortunate destiny to live through the hurried show-trial of the Mughal Badshah followed by the latter's banishment to Burma.

If the Uprising was a rude assault on the placid city as Ghalib knew it, its aftermath was a study in the faceless barbarity of the conquerors, let loose with cold, calculated aplomb to punish Delhi and its citizens. Mirza Nausha lived through the cataclysm and recounted it in his letters, trying to make sense of it. His heart recoiled at the mass hangings in Chandni Chowk and other parts of the city, the wanton burning of homes and property, the wholesale devastation. Libraries were desecrated, presses and bookshops vandalised and madrasas shut down. Precious books and manuscripts were destroyed, so much so that Ghalib lost much of his own life's work. He had never kept copies of his writings, and the two private libraries that were conscientious in their safekeeping of his verses, were torn down.

He writes in a letter that a faqir with a good singing voice

---

[176]Hali was one of his favourite pupils and later wrote a comprehensive biography of Ghalib, *Yaadgaar-e-Ghalib*.

found his (Ghalib's) ghazal somewhere and got it written down on a piece of paper, then showed it to the poet at some point. 'I tell you ... tears came to my eyes...' ends Mirza on a pathetic note. He aged sooner with the terrible torment of those years, when, in his words, 'the whole city became a desert'.

It's hardly surprising that in 1863, he was seriously affected by the Delhi Sore. Boils erupted on his hands and legs, and he suffered terribly even though he received modern Western-style medical treatment. After a protracted recovery, he was finally able to walk again, but with the help of a stick. His eyesight and hearing also deteriorated. During a return journey from Rampur to Delhi in January 1866, he met with an accident and that exacerbated his frail condition. By 1867, his old afflictions, like colic, had begun to flare up alarmingly and his health declined even more. His hearing had gone and his memory was beginning to fail. His liver was a source of agony, but he continued to consume small amounts of alcohol as per his lifelong habit. Nonetheless, he remained mentally alert and pupils kept badgering him with their work to which he continued to respond as well as he could. Finally in late 1867, in sheer desperation, he put out a plea in newspapers to the effect that he was now old and ill and still poems continued to pour in for correction; he pleaded for respite. But nothing changed; the ghazals kept coming and Ghalib kept up his attempts to correct them.

For many years now, Ghalib's near total destitution had driven him to moneylenders for even the household's daily needs. He was now anxious to repay his creditors because he knew that there was no way to do that after his death. In fact, the poet's greatest worry was how his wife would survive and manage household finances after he was gone.

A few days before his death, Muhammad Hussain Hali paid him a visit. When Hali came, Ghalib was dictating a reply to a letter from Nawab Alauddin Khan of Loharu who had been his pupil. 'You ask me how I am... Ask my neighbours after two or three days!' The end came on 15 February 1869. Ghalib was buried in the family cemetery of the Loharu family.[177] His wife Umrao died exactly a year later. Mirza Ghalib's legacy lives on in Ballimaran and Chandni Chowk, then extends far beyond the storied streets of Delhi, to encircle the whole wide world of Urdu adab that knows no borders.

Further readings on Mirza Ghalib:

1. Farooqi, Mehr Afshan, *Ghalib: A Wilderness at my Doorstep: A Critical Biography*, Penguin Allen Lane, 2021.
2. Jung, Najeeb (trans.), *Deewan-e-Ghalib: Sariir-e-Khaama*, Delhi: Rekhta Foundation, 2021.
3. Mir, Raza, *Ghalib: A Thousand Desires*, Gurgaon: Penguin Books India, 2019.
4. Narang, Gopi Chand (trans. Surinder Deol), *Ghalib: Innovative Meanings and the Ingenious Mind*, New Delhi: Oxford University Press, 2017.
5. Russell, Ralph (ed.), *The Oxford India Ghalib: Life, Letters and Ghazals*, New Delhi: Oxford University Press, 2007.

[177]Mirza Ghalib's grave lies in present-day Basti Nizamuddin, Delhi. An interesting story about his grave is that it lay forgotten and was poorly kept till 1954 when the film *Mirza Ghalib* was released. Produced by Sohrab Modi and written by Saadat Hasan Manto, the film stirred popular imagination, and was also screened at the Rashtrapati Bhavan where President Rajendra Prasad and Jawaharlal Nehru watched it along with other dignitaries. Nehru was deeply moved and remarked to Sohrab Modi, 'You've brought Ghalib back to life!'

The film did good business and it is believed that Sohrab Modi got the grave renovated with his own money. On a side note, while the film continued to draw huge crowds in Ghalib's Delhi, Saadat Hasan Manto died in Lahore on 18 January 1955.

Another great poet of the subcontinent, Allama Mohammad Iqbal, who visited the grave way back in 1905, believed that coming to Ghalib's grave was equivalent to a pilgrimage. *https://thepatriot.in/heritage/why-ghalib-was-buried-so-far-away-from-his-abode-44034*

Sheikh Mohammad Ibrahim Zauq (1789–1854)

Mohammad Ibrahim Zauq had humble beginnings by all accounts. Despite this, he rose to uncharted heights on account of his unmatched brilliance in Urdu poetry. As Poet Laureate of the last Mughal court of Bahadur Shah Zafar and as his ustad, Zauq became first among equals. Beyond the Qila, he was at the centre of a vibrant literary universe consisting of Delhi's elite, his peers, friends and scores of admirers and pupils. Simultaneously, he had a famously fractious relationship with his celebrated contemporary, Mirza Ghalib, with whom he had several well-publicised disputes and disagreements. He also taught Daagh Dehlvi, the accomplished shagird and one of the last classical Urdu poets whose ghazals are sung to this day. Ustad Zauq was not only a master poet whose contribution to the Delhi Renaissance was immeasurable, but he was also one of the last great icons of the rich cultural life of Delhi in the mid-nineteenth century.

In 1789 CE, near Kabuli Gate in the heart of Delhi, a son was born to Sheikh Mohammad Ramzan, a poor soldier who had travelled from Shahpur in Uttar Pradesh to Delhi in search of employment. Zauq was Mohammad Ramzan's only son. When he was old enough to study, Zauq was sent to Hafiz Ghulam Rasul, a Quran reciter living near his house. Hafiz Ghulam Rasul had an affinity for poetry and wrote under the pen name 'Shauq'. Not content with penning verses himself, Shauq also ignited a love for poetry in his pupils, encouraging them to read earlier masters as well as write verses themselves. And so, there pervaded in the madrasa an atmosphere of poetic appreciation and enthusiasm. The student Zauq memorised verses of Urdu masters, and fervently prayed to God that he might also become a great poet one day.

Muhammad Husain Azad states in *Aab-e hayat* that the first two verses that Zauq wrote in childhood were a hamd (verse in praise of God) and a na'‘t (verse in praise of the Prophet Muhammad). As a young boy, he was hardly able to ‘read’ this as an auspicious omen, but later in life, Zauq would recount how his heart had overflowed with delight after he had crafted these debut verses. He wrote them over and over again, in his notebooks and other places, in different colours and variously embellished.

After finishing school with Hafiz Ghulam Rasul, Zauq enrolled at another madrasa for further education. This was where he came under the mentorship of Shah Nasir, a well-known poet and teacher of Delhi and whom everyone knew as Kaale saheb. Kaale saheb was ustad to the royal princes and to Momin Khan. He was also close to Mirza Ghalib and the Mughal Badshah.

Zauq's introduction to Shah Nasir was through Mir Kazim Husain Beqaraar, a close friend. One day, Beqaraar composed a verse that impressed Zauq. When he asked Beqaraar about this composition that was decidedly superior to his earlier work, Beqaraar informed him that he had recently been accepted as a shagird by Shah Nasir. Upon Zauq's request, Beqaraar introduced him to Shah Nasir, and very quickly, Zauq became Nasir's favourite pupil. His former ustad Shauq was not too pleased, but that did not deter Zauq from continuing his apprenticeship under Shah Nasir.

Soon Zauq was confidently scaling greater heights, and he did not feel the need to show all his work to Shah Nasir for revision. Where he used to accompany his ustad to mushairas not so long ago, he now began attending them on his own. His arc of inspiration took him to earlier masters like Mirza Sauda, and one day, he composed a ghazal on one of Sauda's ghazals. In literary circles, this is a well-accepted practice, and to compose a ghazal on a previous master's work is a graceful tribute to the master. When the young Zauq showed his ghazal to Shah Nasir, however, the latter grew annoyed and berated Zauq for overreaching and trying to fly too close to the sun, in this case, the great Mirza Muhammad Rafi Sauda. Zauq went away crestfallen.

Confused and disappointed, a storm raging in his heart, he went to the Jama Masjid for his prayers. Afterward, he met Meer Kallu Haqir at the pool in the courtyard. Now, even as an upcoming poet, Zauq was well recognised in the city because of his lively readings at mushairas. When Meer saheb asked why he seemed downcast, Zauq confided in him. Meer saheb in turn was all compassion; he encouraged the young poet to go ahead and recite the ghazal without any misgivings. He invoked a lot of blessings for the young Zauq and thus restored his floundering spirit.[178]

Zauq's presence at mushairas was thrilling, his recitation energetic, and senior poets praised his work generously. Zauq's fame was now spilling into the streets and his ghazals were on everyone's lips.

During the reign of Akbar Shah II, Zauq came to be associated with the Qila and the Mughal court. This was when Bahadur Shah Zafar was Wali Ahad or Crown Prince. Zafar was passionate about Urdu poetry and a poet of merit himself; he held regular mehfils to bring together the poets of Delhi. Beqaraar was one of his personal courtiers; through him, Zauq got the opportunity to attend the court of the Crown Prince. By around 1807, Zauq was a regular visitor to the Qila. During the course of his visits, Zauq was able to impress Zafar with his quick-wittedness and slick versification, and the latter appointed Zauq as his ustad

[178]*https://dsal.uchicago.edu/books/PK2155.H8413/420442d5.html*

at a monthly remuneration of four rupees. Ustad Zauq was less than twenty years old at the time.

The Emperor Akbar Shah II was also dazzled by Zauq's poetic talent after the latter wrote a qasidah in his praise. As a reward, Akbar Shah conferred upon Zauq the title of Khaqaani-e-Hind (Khaqaani of Hindustan). There could have been no greater honour for Zauq than to be compared thus with Khaqaani, the illustrious twelfth-century Persian poet born in Shirvan, Iran, himself a child prodigy and famous for his qasidahs.

Akbar Shah II died in 1837 and Bahadur Shah Zafar succeeded him as Badshah. Zauq composed a magnificent qasidah for his coronation. He was now appointed Malik-ush-Shora or Poet Laureate. Despite this elevation in the court's hierarchy, however, Zauq's monthly salary remained stagnant at four rupees. Zauq never complained. Later, his monthly remuneration was increased to thirty rupees and then to a respectable hundred rupees a month. It is entirely plausible that these monetary enhancements did not matter much to the poet when weighed against the Badshah's veneration of him. In turn, Zauq was devoted to the Emperor. He knew that his position in the Qila boosted his standing among the cultured elite of the city. All the while, he continued to reside in his modest house at Kabuli Darwaza and kept to his disciplined and religious way of living. At the same time, he enjoyed the privileges of his rank, moving around the city in royal style in a palanquin with bearers.

Zauq was dark complexioned and bright-eyed, with smallpox marks on his face, but they did not detract from his overall pleasant look. Of average height, he had a brisk walk, a general quickness of body and a pleasing voice that he employed with great effect for recitations at mushairas. He had a sharp temperament and a remarkable memory. Armed with an impressive understanding of a range of subjects like art, history and Quranic commentaries, he was seen as a wellspring of knowledge. He was also God-fearing and deeply devoted to the Prophet Muhammad. It was his custom to visit the shrine at Dargah Qadam Shareef in Paharganj every Thursday, spending time in silent contemplation. Gifted with a naturally curious mind, Ustad Zauq had many diverse accomplishments. At one point, his interest turned to music and he gained some proficiency in it, but he quit when he realised that for total mastery, music required the commitment of a far greater length of time and a single-minded focus. He also learnt astrology and geomancy under a teacher, but again, he lost heart when his astrology teacher informed him that it would take seventy-seven years to learn about every star and its range of influence.

Ustad Zauq's poetry displays a great facility for language, and he is known for his brilliant employment of commonly spoken Urdu phrases and colloquialisms. In a qasidah he composed for Akbar Shah, for instance, he had crafted eighteen couplets in eighteen different languages or dialects. His poetry, therefore, is seen as an authentic reflection of the language as it lived and breathed in that epoch. His compositions span the spectrum of forms: ghazals, masnavis, qasidahs, chronograms. However, not much survives of his copious output. His collection of verses, *Diwan-e-Zauq*, was published by his favourite pupil Muhammad Husain Azad, who managed to save Ustad Zauq's manuscript even as he was forced to leave his home in the midst of the inferno raging in Delhi in late 1857.

Azad writes:

> My situation was that the soldiers of the victorious army suddenly entered the house. They flourished their rifles: 'Leave here at once!' The world turned black before my eyes. A whole houseful of goods was before me, and I stood petrified: 'What shall I take with me?' My eye fell on the big bundle of the Ustad's (Zauq) ghazals. I thought,

> 'Muhammad Husain, if God is gracious, and you live, then everything can be restored. But where will this very Ustad come from, who can compose these ghazals again? Now only his name lives. If his name has life, then it is only because of these. While these exist, he lives even after his death; if these are lost, his name cannot survive either.' I picked up the bundle and tucked it under my arm.[179]

Ustad Zauq did, however, carefully oversee the publication of the verses of his shagird, Badshah Bahadur Shah. A few years after Zafar was crowned, his first divan came out in 1845, and by the 1850s, three more divans were published (a set of four divans comprising the *Diwan-e Huzur-e Vaala* edition). Obviously, this took up a lot of Zauq's time and energy, and consequently, he was unable to focus on putting together his own work.[180]

No account of Sheikh Ibrahim Zauq can be complete without touching upon his combative relationship with Mirza Ghalib, nine years his junior in age. Zauq, with his penchant for prim correctness in grammar and in personal conduct, frowned upon Ghalib's free-format ways. Ghalib, the highbrow non-conformist, did not think much of Zauq's poetry and was resentful of his position at the Mughal court. The two were caught in a constant battle of wits and words.

In December 1851, on the occasion of the marriage of Bahadur Shah Zafar's son, Prince Jawan Bakht, the two titans locked horns yet again. Jawan Bakht's mother, Zinat Mahal, was the Emperor's favourite wife, and Zafar was keen to get the British to recognise Jawan Bakht as the Crown Prince even though the boy was younger than his other sons. Naturally then, the young prince's marriage had been planned on a grand scale for greater effect, and the city was buzzing with excitement. Zinat Mahal

---

[179] Azad, *Aab-e hayat, https://dsal.uchicago.edu/books/PK2155.H8413/442457d5.html*

[180] Amar Farooqui, *Zafar and the Raj: Anglo-Mughal Delhi, c. 1800-1850*, p. 117.

asked Ghalib to write a sehra[181] for the occasion, which he did. And he could not also resist adding a couplet that was deliberately provocative and clearly aimed at Ustad Zauq.

Now the Badshah did not appreciate his teacher being in Ghalib's crosshairs in this way. He encouraged Zauq to respond in a befitting manner. Zauq wrote his poetic response, questioning Ghalib's ability to challenge him. It was hardly surprising that Zauq's response was given a lot of publicity and was even published in the next day's local newspaper. It was now Ghalib's turn to think. Initially, Ghalib had thought that it was only Zauq whom he had annoyed, but seeing the wide publicity being accorded to Zauq's rejoinder, it was clear as day that the Badshah was also irked with his impudence. Keeping his tone remorseful, Ghalib penned an apology for having crossed an invisible boundary. Then again, typical of Ghalib, the apology-verse contained double entendre, and thinly veiled disdain for Zauq's humble origins, his own proud lineage in contrast and his masterful grasp of Persian, the language of the kings of yore, and so it went.

Who is to say if Badshah Zafar actually got mollified with Ghalib's apology or not. Whatever the answer to that, what's certain is that Delhi's citizens derived a lot of entertainment from this spat, and it remained a 'trending topic' for weeks! Social media channels of the time, wandering musicians, poetry enthusiasts and others played no small part in amplifying both poets' voices.

Zauq remained the Badshah's ustad and Poet Laureate of the court for full seventeen years, and during this time, it is believed he wrote more than three hundred and fifty ghazals and about sixty qasidahs in honour of Akbar Shah II and Bahadur Shah Zafar.

Zauq died in 1854. He was spared the agony and heartache

---

[181]In popular South Asian tradition, a sehra is sung at a wedding, praising the groom and praying to God for his future wedded life. It is especially popular in Uttar Pradesh and Hyderabad.

of living through the Uprising and its disastrous fallout, unlike Ghalib. In early October 1854, he came down with a fever and a gastrointestinal disorder, finally succumbing on 18 October 1854. It was entirely unexpected and Delhi went into deep shock and mourning. Even Ghalib sank into a state of depression and sorrow. The Emperor wanted Zauq to be interred in the royal cemetery within the Qila, but Zauq had earlier expressed his wish to be buried near his favourite place, Dargah Qadam Shareef,[182] and that was where he was put to rest.

Many years ago, the ustad had gone to visit a blind astrologer named Pandit Tulsi Ram in Makkhan Lal Ganj. After a stimulating conversation on a range of topics, Zauq mentioned the details of his own horoscope, but did not disclose that it was his, to be able to get a candid prediction. The astrologer made a prediction that the person in question would be greatly accomplished in some art, and that it would bring him fame and recognition. He would have many opponents too, but none would be able to stand before him. Ustad Zauq then asked, 'How long will this person live?' The astrologer said, 'Sixty-seven or sixty-eight years; the limit is sixty-nine.'[183]

An untimely death at the age of sixty-five ultimately parted Ustad Ibrahim Zauq from the streets of his beloved Delhi, a city he could never imagine leaving in his lifetime.

He wrote the following verse at a time when many artistes and poets were leaving Delhi and making a beeline for Hyderabad in the Deccan in search of brighter prospects:

in dinoN garche dakkan meiN hai bohat qadr-e-sukhan
kaun jaae Zauq par Dilli ki galiyaan chhoD kar

---

[182]Located in the Nabi Karim area of Paharganj, Delhi, his grave, unfortunately, lies in a dilapidated state today.

[183]This incident is recounted in part seven of *Aab-e hayat*, *https://dsal.uchicago.edu/books/PK2155.H8413/442457d5.html*

These days Urdu poetry enjoys much prestige in Deccan
But really, Zauq, who wants to leave the lanes of Dehli.

A few hours before his death, Zauq had penned these lines:

kehte haiN aaj Zauq jahaaN se guzar gayaa
kya KHoob aadmi tha, Khuda maGfirat kare

They say Zauq has passed on from this world today
What a man... may God forgive his sins!

Further reading on Sheikh Ibrahim Zauq (in Hindi):

1. Sharma, O. P. (ed.) *Zauq*, Bhopal: Manjul Publishing House, 2019.

Hakim Momin Khan Momin (1800–1852)

Momin Khan was born in 1800 in Kucha Chelan, Delhi. His grandfather and granduncle, both Unani physicians, had migrated from Kashmir to Delhi during the reign of Alam Shah II (1759–1806 CE). The name 'Momin', meaning 'believer in Islam', was given to him by his father's teacher, Shah Abdul Aziz Dehlvi. His family wanted to call him Habibullah, but eventually Momin was the name that he came to be known by.

Momin's father was an intellectual and he ensured that alongside a training in medicine, his son's education was equally well-grounded in religion and languages like Arabic and Persian. It's hardly surprising then that this scion of a wealthy and educated family stood in a class of his own as the most stylish and sophisticated master poet of nineteenth-century Delhi.

Hakim Momin Khan was singularly gifted in diagnosing ailments and relieving his patients' complaints. He trained under his father Hakim Ghulam Nabi Khan, and thereafter, became a much sought after hakim acclaimed for his miraculous healing touch. Momin Khan believed that this was a divinely blessed calling and never charged any fee for his prescriptions and treatments.

Momin was also blessed with a phenomenal memory. As a child, when he was learning Arabic from Shah Abdul Qadir, he was able to remember every word his teacher spoke. And, after hearing a sermon by Shah Abdul Aziz Dehlvi, he could repeat it word for word. His excellent recall turned out to be a great asset when later in life, his enquiring mind led him to the study of astrology. Muhammad Husain Azad elaborates:

> He had a natural affinity for astrology. He attained such expertise that when they heard his pronouncements, great astrologers were astonished. In the course of a year, he looked one time at the almanac. Then all the positions of the stars and the state of their movements for every day of the year remained in his mind. When someone placed a question before him, he neither drew a horoscope nor looked at the almanac. He said to the inquirer, 'Be silent. Whatever I ask you, just answer me.' Then he asked various things, and the interrogator usually accepted his word.[184]

Chess was another one of his passions. When he sat down to play a game, he grew oblivious of everything else around him. Azad states that there were only one or two other chess players in the city who were better than Momin Khan. That was not all, he was also a good singer and an accomplished flautist. But it was his poetry that made him immortal. He began writing at the age of sixteen under Shah Nasir, popularly known as Kaale saheb. After a while, however, he stopped obtaining corrections from Shah Nasir as his own instincts became the guiding force to fulfil the promise of his growing poetic sensibility.

Momin led a comfortable life, owing largely to the pension his ancestors had been granted by the British government and that he had inherited, as well as the annuity from the British Crown. He was good looking, with large pensive eyes and long curly hair, and he dressed fashionably, his love for fine clothes a well-known fact among the city elite.

Momin Khan had a series of romantic relationships with women;

---

[184]This is mentioned in part five of *Aab-e hayat*, *https://dsal.uchicago.edu/books/PK2155.H8413/404419d5.html*

among these, a courtesan from Lucknow, Ummul Fatima, stands out. She visited Delhi sometime in the 1820s and was staying at a house in Kucha Chelan. As it happened, she suffered from a minor bout of fever, and the famous hakim was summoned to treat her. Momin Khan fell in love with her hennaed hands as he felt her pulse from beyond the purdah. The affair, however, soon came to be publicised and the lady in question returned to Lucknow. Thereafter, he fell in love with a girl from Rampur, and ended up traveling to Rampur frequently to meet her. At the age of twenty-three, Momin was married to the daughter of a rural zamindar. The marriage did not last, most likely because his wife was too traditional or could not live up to his expectations. He married again, this time to an educated woman from the distinguished family of Khwaja Mir Dard. This was a happy relationship and he was well integrated with his wife's family.

Meanwhile, Momin Khan's poetry flourished; his passion and flair ensured his galvanising presence at all mushairas held in the city. His soulful style of recitation would be greeted with deep appreciation, evocative as it was with the movement of his fingers through his curly tresses and the subtle rhythmic intonation of his voice. He also had several students, a few of them recognised poets in their own right. Nawab Mustafa Khan Shefta, one of his pupils and a celebrated poet, published Momin's complete works in 1843 as *Kulliyat-e Momin*. A divan of his Persian poetry was also published around the same time.

Interestingly, one does not find among his works any qasidahs or odes in praise of royal personalities, as was the common practice then among poets associated with courts and royalty. Muhammad Azad recounts that the Maharaja of Kapurthala offered Momin Khan the position of Poet Laureate at a monthly salary of three hundred and fifty rupees. He even sent a thousand rupees for the poet's travel expenses from Delhi to Kapurthala. But when the poet learned that a singer at the Maharaja's court earned the same amount, he turned down the offer.

There is another anecdote about how Ajeet Singh, the brother of the Maharaja of Patiala, gifted Momin Khan an elephant after the two had spent a wonderful evening together filled with exquisite poetry. It was a token of Ajeet Singh's lavish appreciation. Poor Momin Khan, he tried to escape being saddled with this giant trophy by saying he was a poor man and would not be able to look after the elephant. Without batting an eyelid, Ajeet Singh gave him a hundred rupees for its upkeep. Momin Khan had little choice now but to go home with the mastodon. Nevertheless, he lost no time in getting rid of the unusual pet! At the same time, out of courtesy and to repay Ajeet Singh's favour, he composed a few verses for him.

Like most Delhi poets, Momin Khan loved Delhi and would not easily agree to be parted from it. Around 1841, he was offered a lecturer's position at the Delhi College by his friend James Thomason, an administrator of the East India Company, at a salary of eighty rupees a month. Momin demanded a hundred. Thomason agreed, but on the condition that the poet would occasionally have to travel with him outside of Delhi. This was quite out of the question for Momin, and he rejected the position with the retort that he would not 'sell Delhi' for a hundred rupees. A proud and sensitive man, he never used his accomplishments in astrology, geomancy and his practice of medicine as means of livelihood. Poetry remained sacrosanct above all else.

Momin Khan shared a warm friendship with Mirza Ghalib, and in 1847, when Ghalib was thrown into prison for gambling, Momin Khan stood by his side like a rock: attempting to bail him out, helping his family and doing all he could to ease the situation for Ghalib.

True to the name he had been given by his father's teacher, Momin was a pious and devout Muslim. At the same time, he was also a diehard romantic, nursing a tender lover's heart. His iridescent poetry found its shoots in the cracks between the two facets of his persona. It is a well-known fact that Mirza Ghalib, not just a great friend but also an admirer of his poetry, had once expressed a wish to trade his entire divan for one of Momin's creations, so enchanted was he with this diamond of a sher:

tum mere paas hote ho goya
jab koi duusra nahiiN hota

You remain with me
When nobody else is there.

This deceptively simple sher gleams with the use of the word 'goya', meaning 'as if'. Multiple interpretations are possible, a galaxy of possibilities is seen and Ghalib was mesmerised by it.

In 1852, when Momin Khan was in the prime of life, he lost his footing on the terrace of his home where he was supervising some repair work. He fell to the ground and sustained serious injuries. He died within five days, on 14 May 1852. He was laid to rest in the graveyard at Mehdiyan, situated near present-day Maulana Azad Medical College, Delhi.

His unexpected and tragic death came as a terrible shock not only to his friends and peers, but to the entire city. Ghalib was shattered and broken-hearted. In a letter to a friend, he wrote how Momin and he had befriended each other when they were mere boys of fourteen or fifteen, and how they'd never had any falling out in all the decades they had spent together.

Momin Khan is probably not at the forefront of our collective memory today; it is Ghalib who rules popular imagination more than any other poet. But Momin Khan's fine ghazals with their delicate touch and gossamer wordplay remain alive and well among Urdu poetry lovers...and Momin in some paradise would be content, that his poetry lives on in his cherished Delhi.

Further readings on Momin Khan Momin (in Hindi):

1. Ehsaas, Farhat (ed.), *Rekhta ke Momin (Rekhta Classics)*. Delhi: Rajkamal Prakashan, Rekhta Books, 2021.
2. Sharma, O. P. (ed.) *Momin*, Bhopal: Manjul Publishing House, 2019.

Glossary of select terms

Angrakha: A long tunic or coat for men, like an achkan, open on the side and covering the chest, with long sleeves sometimes cut from the front for rolling up. There were separate ones for summer and winter, with the summer ones being made from muslin and light fabrics, and the winter ones being lined with soft cotton.

Baithak: A meeting hall or a small area for congregating; a sitting room for formal and informal get togethers.

Bismillah: An Arabic word meaning 'In the name of the Almighty'. It is a benediction, often invoked before the start of an event or action.

Bazm-e-urdu: An assembly or gathering of Urdu speakers and others deeply interested in the language. It could be a wide-ranging group, and is not limited to only Urdu poets and poetry.

Chau-goshia: A Mughal style of pagri or turban, divided into four segments, mounted on a wooden frame and embellished with heavy embroidery.

Chobdaar: A mace bearer or herald carrying a staff, sometimes golden or silver, and walking in front of nobles or members of royalty, to announce them. The presence of a chobdaar signified rank.

Gao-takiya: A bolster; a long cylindrical pillow used as a backrest.

Haaziriin: Gathered, those assembled (in the plural).

Hafiz: One who has memorised the Quran; also called Hafiz-e-Quran. Hafiz is also a protector or a guardian or a preserver, as in 'Khuda hafiz'. It also means someone with a good memory.

Haveli, kothi: A haveli is a large, spacious house probably with multiple stories and several rooms. The term kothi was used to describe a house that had an amalgamation of the traditional Indian and British architectural features, for instance, a central courtyard and enclosed rooms built in the British fashion.

Ibtada: The start or beginning of a thing or event or sequence of action; the first step. The word is of Arabic origin.

Inteha: An Arabic-origin word referring to the extreme or final limit.

Inshallah: An Arabic word meaning 'God willing'; a prayerful wish that has no true English equivalent. It has a notion of expressing a wish or intention that the universe in its mercy might deem fit to fulfil.

Islah: Correction, revision or improvement. It is used largely in the context of an apprentice poet or writer seeking guidance or getting revisions (islah lena) from their ustad or teacher.

Kalaam: A work of poetry, a collection of verses. For a deeper exploration of the word and its range of interpretations, please visit *https://rekhtadictionary.com/meaning-of-kalaam*.

Kewra: The essence of the pandanus or screw pine plant and its flowers that has a pleasant fragrance. It is used in sweets and foodstuffs.

Khaas-daan: A container made of silver (or sometimes copper) with a dome-shaped cover to keep betel leaves.

Mardana or Mardaan-Khana: Usually located in the front part of a house with easy access to the exterior, this was the male section where the men met their peers, pupils and others.

Masnad: Royal seat of honour; a throne; a seat made of a large comfortable cushion.

Masnavi: A series of distichs (couplets) in rhymed pairs (*aa*, *bb*, *cc*, and so on) that constitutes a characteristic type of Persian verse. It is used mostly for heroic, historical and romantic epic poetry.

Matla, maqta: Matla is the opening rhyming couplet of a ghazal or a qasidah, and maqta, the last couplet in which the pen name of the poet appears.

Misra: A single line of a poem.

Nausha: A bridegroom or a young king.

Nishast: A place for sitting or assembling; a seat; a gathering or assembly.

Qasidah: A genre of Urdu and Persian poetry in praise of a person; a eulogy or an ode. It is usually a long poem with an elaborate metre and rhyme scheme and has its origins in Arabic. A qasidah-go or qasidah-nigaar is a poet writing qasidahs.

Qafiya: The rhyme or metre; the last syllable in a couplet to which all couplets rhyme. In a ghazal, the penultimate syllable is called the qafiya.

Radiif: The word or group of words that are repeated after the rhyme in a ghazal or qasidah. In a completely different context, it also means the person sitting behind the main rider on a horse or camel, or the army that follows behind.

In these couplets by Tishna, the qafiya is 'KHabar', 'sehar' and the radiif is 'kuchh bhi nahiiN':

aaNkh paDti hai kahiiN, paanv kahiiN paDta hai
sab ki hai tumko KHabar, apni KHabar kuchh bhi nahiiN

shama hai, gul bhi hai, bulbul bhi hai, parvanaa bhi
raat ki raat yeh sab kuchh hai, sehar kuchh bhi nahiiN

Rekhta: The old name for Urdu or the mixed language sometimes also referred to as Hindustani. Also, a poetic form in which ghazals are crafted using a mix of Farsi and Hindi.

Rubai: A form of poetry in which a theme is expressed through four hemistichs. It originated in Iran and was made famous by Omar Khayyam and his Persian quatrains. It is composed in twenty-four syllables, with its first, second and fourth hemistichs following the same rhyming elements. For more, please visit *https://www.rekhtadictionary.com/meaning-of-rubaaii-1*.

Saheb-e-alam: A mode of address for a prince.

Salle-'alaa: An Arabic benediction meaning 'peace be upon the Prophet Muhammad'. It is used as a benediction, a blessing in appreciation.

Sehra: A kind of veil made of fragrant flowers, such as jasmine, and tied around the forehead to cover the face of the bride or the bridegroom during a traditional Indian marriage ceremony. It is also a genre of songs sung during a marriage ceremony.

Shab-e-hijr: A night of separation, especially from the beloved. Much ink has been spilt in exploring this theme in Persian and Urdu poetry. In this couplet, Aazurda has a deeply moving experience of shab-e-hijr:

kaTti kisi tarah bhi nahiiN yeh shab-e-firaaq
shaayad ke gardish aaj tujhe aasmaaN nahiiN

This night of separation does not seem to pass, no matter how I try
Maybe the heavens hesitate in their revolution tonight.

Shagird: A pupil or an apprentice; sometimes a religious disciple.

Shehzada: A prince; the son of a king or a badshah.

Subhan-allah: An expression of deep appreciation meaning 'God be praised!', 'Praise to Allah!', 'Well done!'.

Takhallus: The pen name of a poet. Sometimes, poets took separate pen names for their compositions in different languages.

Tehzeeb: Civilisation, culture and prevalent social mores.

Wali Ahad: The heir apparent or the crown prince.

Wazir-e-azam: The prime minister.

Zenana or mahalsara: Zenana was the female apartment inside the house, not accessible to everyone. Even the menfolk of the family could only come in at set times during the day, and had to ask before entering.

Bibliography

English sources:

Azad, Muhammad Husain (trans.) and Frances W. Pritchett (ed.) in association with Shamsur Rahman Faruqi, *Aab-e Hayat: Shaping the Canon of Urdu Poetry*, DSAL version, 2005, https://dsal.uchicago.edu/books/PK2155.H8413/index.html#top

Baig, Mirza Farhatullah (trans.) Akhtar Qamber, *The Last Mushai'rah of Dehli* (PB), New Delhi: Orient Blackswan Pvt. Ltd., 2010. First published in 1979 by Orient Longman Pvt. Ltd.

Dalrymple, William, *White Mughals: Love and Betrayal in Eighteenth-century India*, Gurgaon: Penguin Books, 2004.

Dalrymple, William, *The Last Mughal: The Fall of a Dynasty, Delhi, 1857*, Gurgaon: Penguin Books, 2007.

Farooqui, Amar, *Zafar and the Raj: Anglo-Mughal Delhi c. 1800-1850*, Delhi: Primus Books, 2013.

Faruqi, Shamsur Rahman, *The Mirror of Beauty*, Gurgaon: Penguin Books, 2014.

Gupta, Narayani, *Delhi between Two Empires 1803-1931*, New Delhi: Oxford India Paperbacks, 1998.

Mahmood, Saif, *Beloved Delhi: A Mughal City and Her Greatest Poets*, New Delhi: Speaking Tiger, 2018.

Mahmudabad, Ali Khan, *Poetry of Belonging: Muslim Imaginings of India 1850-1950*, New Delhi: Oxford University Press, 2020.

Munshi Faizuddin (trans.) Ather Farouqui, *The Last Gathering: A Vivid Portrait of Life in the Red Fort*, New Delhi: Roli Books (Lotus Collection), 2021.

Nasr, Seyyed Hossein (editor-in-chief), *The Study Quran: A New Translation and Commentary*, New York: HarperCollins Publishers, 2015.

Nizami, K.A. (trans.) Ather Farouqui, *Delhi in Historical Perspectives*, New Delhi: Oxford University Press, 2020.

Parvez, Aslam (trans.) Ather Farouqui, *The Life and Poetry of Bahadur Shah Zafar*, New Delhi: Hay House India, 2021.

Pritchett, Frances W., *Nets of Awareness: Urdu Poetry and its Critics* (South Asian edition), New Delhi: Katha, 2004.

Safvi, Rana (trans.), *City of my Heart: Accounts of Love, Loss and Betrayal in Nineteenth-century Delhi*, Gurugram: Hachette India, 2018.

Spear, Percival, *Twilight of the Mughuls: Studies in Late Mughul Delhi*, New Delhi: Munshiram Manoharlal Pvt. Ltd., 1991.

Varma, Pavan K., *Ghalib: The Man, the Times*, Gurgaon: Penguin Books India, 2008.

Urdu sources:

Farouqui, Ather (ed.), *Rasheed Hasan Khan: Shakhsiyat aur adabi Khidmaat*, New Delhi: Maktaba Jamia, 2002.

Farzana, Ruhi, *Mirza Farhatullah Baig: Hayat aur Fann*, New Delhi: Modern Publishing House, 2013.

Hashmi, Rafiuddin (ed.), *Mazameen-e Farhatullah Baig (Intekhab)*. https://www.rekhta.org/ebooks/mazameen-e-farhatullah-beg-intekhab-ebooks

Acknowledgements

This book was born during the pandemic with all its unreality, its painful uncertainty. Working on it was an act of faith that took me to a place where I would lose myself for hours on end. But to move beyond that stage to the actual publishing of the book was a long journey, and I'm indebted to the people who made it possible, and without whom I would have floundered.

I owe a deep debt of gratitude to Dr Ather Farouqui for his unflagging support and guidance through successive stages of this work, right from the first step to the writing of the Foreword. It was also my good fortune to be able to gain access to the exceptional ATUH library for invaluable Urdu works.

Heartfelt shukriya to Dr Baidar Bakht, Member of the Order of Canada and renowned Urdu scholar and translator, for making the time to go through the entire manuscript and for several insightful suggestions that helped me refine the final translation.

Jaya Bhattacharji Rose (Ace Literary Consulting) was the among the first people to believe in the value of this work, and for her backing, her friendship, and for our cherished late-evening long conversations, I remain ever grateful.

To Dr Shah Alam Khan and Rana Safvi who went through the manuscript and gave helpful comments—my sincere gratitude. Dr Shah Alam Khan lent a hand to enhance the mushaira's magic with his suggestion to include the Urdu ghazals.

I owe a special word of thanks to Amaryllis, and especially Bidisha Srivastava, for her close attention to the little things that make a big difference.

My son Utkarsh and husband Abhay gave me their unfailing support and encouragement, and shored me up during my dark, diffident patches—and to be sure, there were plenty. Not only did they give me the leeway to lose myself in the lanes of Baig saheb's Dehli, but they also gave me valuable pointers when I felt stuck, especially while working on the Introduction. My gratitude to them goes beyond words.

Finally, and most importantly, my parents, who have always been my strongest champions, and to whom, I owe a debt that I can never repay. Especially to my father and first ustad, who encouraged me to learn Urdu, helped me with its reading, writing, vocabulary, understanding of the finer aspects of Urdu poetry, and much more. And my mother, for all her blessings and duas that gave me invisible wings to venture into unexplored skies. It is to my parents that I dedicate this work.